Magnetic Capital

Raise All The Money You Need For ANY Worthy Venture

Victor J. Menasce

Written by Victor J. Menasce

© Victor J. Menasce, 2017.

Published by CreateSpace, a division of Amazon.com

Cover information:

ISBN-13: 978-1537531588

ISBN-10: 1537531581

DEDICATION

This book is dedicated to my loving wife Nataxja. Thank you for your unwavering support, patience, and love. I'm truly blessed to have you at the center of my life.

.

Table of Contents

ACKNOWLEDGMENTS

So many people have contributed to developing my skills in raising capital. Top of the list is my mother, who taught me about money, managing investments at a very early age. I had the misfortune of losing my mother when I was 18 years old. The investment holding company that she started became my responsibility to manage from 18 years of age. Out of that hardship came a huge learning experience.

Once in the world of business, a huge thank you to my mentors, Adam Choweniac, Murray Goldman, Jim Roche, Rick O'Connor, Terry Matthews, Brian Wilkie, Sam Fuller, Mark McDermott, Pat DiPietro, Christine King and Mike O'Neill.

In recent years, a huge thank you to Mr. George Ross, Mayor Rudi Giuliani, Dr. Nido Qubein,Russell Weigel and Hugh Hilton. Each of you has brought me meaningful depth on some critical aspects of business acquisition and fund raising.

About This Book

This book contains the keys to the kingdom. It is written for the business owner, entrepreneur, business development manager, or civic sector evangelist who is looking to raise money.

Many people consider raising money an inaccessible process that is reserved for Wall Street types who are a special superhuman breed that come from a different gene pool. Others believe that it's possible to raise money, but they feel uncomfortable asking for money, so they don't. Whatever your limiting belief, raising money is the one skill that unlocks you from the financial prison that's holding you back from achieving your goals.

In the world of Magnetic Capital, you're never asking for money. Your approach, your system, your compelling opportunity will feel so natural that raising money will in fact be relatively easy. In the chapters that follow, I will show you the basic principles, strategies, and unravel the human psychology around investing. There are five criteria that need to be met in order to raise money successfully. It's not enough to meet three out of five, or four out of five. You need to meet all five.

Let's be clear, this is no get rich quick scheme. This isn't a trick to manipulate unsuspecting investors with. These pages contain the fundamental fiduciary responsibilities that the top money managers in the world use to raise money every day. It's surprising that very few books have been written on this topic. Perhaps those who possess the knowledge are too busy making money to write books and teach courses.

Foreword by Robert Helms

Money isn't everything. You know that.

But when all that stands between you and a great opportunity is the money, it sure can feel like everything.

You know what it's like. You come across a fantastic opportunity that you just know will be a winner. It's got a great story. The timing is perfect. The market conditions couldn't be better. There's just one problem. You're undercapitalized. Ugh.

For years I've said that if I had waited until I had the money to buy property, I'd only have a few houses. If you think you need to personally come up with all the money to do a deal, you're limiting your results. Great projects always attract capital. In fact, Victor Menasce refers to it as "Magnetic Capital", which is an excellent way to think about it. Sophisticated investors are looking for yield. They want - in fact they need - to put their money to work. And they are often too busy to source opportunities directly. This is where you come in. If your venture is worthy of their capital, they will be drawn to it. In this book, you'll learn how to be sure your projects are compelling enough to get funded.

Having raised capital for years, as well as trained hundreds of people to do the same, I am keenly aware of how hard it can be to ask people for money. But what if there were just a few simple things that could ensure a never-ending supply of funding? The good news is that there are, and the even better news is that you'll find them in the very book you're holding.

You see, Victor has spent years cultivating the distinctions between those who struggle to find money for their projects and those who seem to effortlessly find all the money they need. And he doesn't just talk about it; he's used these very techniques in a variety of industries. Sure, his concepts will work wonders for real estate investors and developers, but they'll also work if you're raising capital for a business, a loan, or even a charity.

The concepts aren't hard to understand. But understanding them isn't the key. Taking action on them is the key. Making them part of your Investor DNA will take focus, effort and long-term perspective. Once you do, you'll never worry about raising capital again.

So, what are you waiting for? Dig in!

To Your Bright Future,

Robert Helms

Host, The Real Estate Guys™ Radio Show

Introduction

What is money? People have a wide emotional relationship with money. For some, money is a score card. For others, money is merely a tool to buy their favorite creature comfort. For a philanthropist, money can be used to save lives or cure disease. For the business owner, money can be used to fund growth.

So what is money? Money is fuel. Whatever your beliefs are, the more money you have, the faster you will go. If you are a spender, you will spend more. If you believe in multiplying money, you will multiply it faster. If you use money to save lives, you will save more lives. Money is just fuel.

For the purpose of this book, we will only consider using money to create an investment rate of return. If your goal is to raise money for a charity, then this book is also for you. If you're looking to get money because you want to spend it, I can't help you. Get a job.

Money can serve multiple purposes simultaneously. It can be used as a growth vehicle, at the same time as for personal enjoyment, at the same time for helping others in need. The balance of these uses depends on your values. These values are deeply personal. My uncle was a stock-broker and a workaholic. He owned a seat on the NY Stock Exchange. He would wake up in the early hours of the morning and trade options and stocks in Asia, then switch to Europe, and then finally grab a coffee to be ready for the opening bell in New York. He spent money on travel, fine art (a Picasso), and he would have dinners catered regularly in his apartment on Fifth Avenue overlooking Central Park. His lifestyle made a huge impression on me as a young child. He had so much more money than my parents, that I aspired to be like him. Now that I'm older, I can see how empty his life really was. He was successful in business, but his life wasn't fulfilling. His psychology determined what he paid attention to. Now that I'm older and have developed my own values rather than trying to copy someone else's, I seek to grow my investment portfolio so that eventually I have the means to make a social impact with my money. If Bill Gates had dedicated his early years to philanthropy instead of growing Microsoft, his impact on the world would have been much less. It was as a result of his massive wealth creation that the Bill and Melinda Gates Foundation has been able to make significant progress towards solving some very big problems that even governments have not attempted.

Success is always the result of a combination of strategy, psychology and execution. All three are necessary. At the foundation of these is psychology. Much of this book will sound like strategy, but is in fact a dissection of the elements that make up the psychology of investing. The human mind can replicate feelings simply through imagination. Fear is quickly associated with pain in many people. People take action to either gain pleasure or avoid pain. Fear is a very powerful motivator. The largest emotion to master is fear. A large part of this book will focus on bringing the tools to accurately analyze a venture. When this happens, fear can be kept in check. Fear can be examined more objectively. We will dissect risk in a structured way that can help quantify risk so that it isn't open ended. Unbounded risk taps into fear at its worst.

None of that matters without execution. There is a step by step approach to breaking down an investor pitch. If you can't communicate it crisply, clearly, concisely and with confidence you won't raise the money.

As you immerse yourself in the chapters that follow, keep one point in mind. All situations vary. These are not hard and fast rules. They're not laws of nature. They vary as much as personalities vary. If you adhere to these methods you will maximize your success as a fundraiser.

Prepare to unlock the vault with the keys to the kingdom.

1 How to Raise Money

Where does investment money come from? Money comes in one of three ways.

1) Earned Income
2) Residual Income
3) Capital Gains

The vast majority of the population work for money. They are trading time or effort for money. If they stop putting in the effort, then the money stops flowing. If they live below their means and manage to save, then they will eventually create a pool of capital to invest. At that point they can start having money work for them rather and working for money.

The problem with saving alone as a way of accumulating wealth is that we live in an inflationary environment. Inflation has the effect of devaluing savings. It has the same effect on debt. Savings alone is a losing game because it offers no leverage. Yes, the government regularly reports on the consumer price index as a measure of inflation. They measure a basket of consumer goods and services as a way determining how quickly prices are rising. In recent years, the consumer price index has been very low. At the same time, interest rates have been extremely low. The combined effects of inflation and earned interest, even with compound interest are negative for savers.

Most of the wealth in the world was created through a combination of residual income and capital gains. There aren't enough hours in a lifetime to generate huge wealth simply by saving employment income alone, even if your hourly rate is high.

Business owners, and owners of income producing assets are the ones who can generate real wealth. These are the 1% that have high incomes and also have amassed wealth. Their wealth comes primarily from residual income and capital gains. These folks can stop working in a traditional job and spend their time managing their investments. These are the accredited investors.

The remainder of the population (the non-accredited investors) have more meager savings that can be aggregated together in larger pools of capital to generate business growth. This is the world of the pension funds, the mutual funds, and retail investment products.

Most other opportunities for business ventures are made available to people who have money to invest.

Who Cares?

Investors don't care about you. They only care about themselves. Lenders and equity investors behave the same way in this regard. They have only one question. "If I give you money, how will I get my return on investment?" They have 50 ways of asking that question, but it boils down to that one single question.

> **"If I give you my money, how will I get my return on investment?"**

If you go to the bank for a loan, they will ask you for lots of documentation.

If I give you my money,
- how will you repay it, along with the interest? (prove your income)
- how have you repaid in the past? (what's your credit score?)
- what is the collateral? (if things go bad)
- what are your other debts? (can you afford it all?)
- what is your income history? (how consistent is your income?)
- will anyone else take it? (do you have any lawsuits?)

You get the idea…

They will be concerned with your credit worthiness. They want to see how you've repaid others in the past as an indication of how you will repay this next loan. They will be concerned with your debt service ratio. This is an indication of your ability to repay the loan. They will be concerned with the loan to value ratio. They want to know that they'll be able to recoup their money in a foreclosure if things go bad. They will be concerned with your track record in managing similar projects. They know that rookies make more mistakes. A strong track record will give them greater confidence that you will meet your projections and obligations.

If you're offering a registered security as a commercial product on the open market, then you can treat the product as a commodity and you will likely never develop a relationship with your investors. The investors will buy a certain number of units in your public stock or mutual fund and their relationship will be with their stock broker or investment dealer who earns a commission on the sale.

We're talking about the world of private equity transactions. These can range in size from a few tens of thousands, to hundreds of millions.

There are five fundamental elements to raising money. Raising money is easy when all five are met, and is exceedingly difficult when one or more is missing.

- Relationship
- Trust
- Results
- Compelling Opportunity
- Alignment

In the chapters that follow, I will break down what is expected in each of these critical areas.

The problem is the all too often the entrepreneur is looking at the problem from their own perspective. In order to connect properly with the money, you need to see it from the other side. Funding partners are not just sources of money to be treated as a commodity.

By truly focusing on addressing these 5 critical elements, raising capital can be actually very easy. But you need to develop the skill, the confidence to have the conversations, and develop a keen eye for assessing the fit between the goals for the project and the goals for the funding partner.

2 - Life as an Entrepreneur

You're probably thinking, "I'm going to be an Entrepreneur? What's an Entrepreneur?" Let's start with a definition. It's actually a French word that is derived from the word "Entre" which means to enter. You're someone who starts new ventures. Much has been written about Entrepreneurship. There are books, magazines, local meet up groups, and university courses as part of an MBA or business program. Generally speaking, entrepreneurs are starting new businesses. You can apply many of the same principles within an existing company. This is sometimes called "Intrapreneurship". For the sake of our discussion, I'm going to assume that you're starting a new venture, regardless whether it's within an existing organization or a new one.

In order to master anything new you require three elements:

1. The knowledge and direction
2. The emotional drive (and eliminate emotional obstacles)
3. The right environment

It's not enough to have one out of three, or two out of three. You must have all three. When you are motivated to become competent, you can often find the information if you search hard enough. But if you're struggling to truly master a skill, there is often an emotional obstacle that is getting in the way. That obstacle might be fear, or perhaps a limiting belief. The psychology of persistence and overcoming emotional obstacles is outside the scope of this book. Steven Pressfield calls this "The Resistance" in his book "The War of Art." Countless other books have been written on the topic of overcoming emotional obstacles.

The most overlooked obstacle is finding the right environment. Most often, even if you're highly motivated, you're usually in the wrong environment. Having a sense of community and connection makes it much easier to navigate the myriad of obstacles that are continually pushing you away from your goal. Environment is the key to becoming an expert. This is true in any discipline. Why do elite athletes from competing countries train for the Olympics together? They need the environment of other elite athletes to develop. An accurate stop watch isn't enough to become a gold medal sprinter. Elite athletes need to be surrounded by coaches and athletes of a similar or higher caliber. Only through discussion, comparison, competition, and collaboration do they improve their skills.

You can read this book, and you'll get a lot of knowledge. You will be a more competent fund raiser after reading this book. But it may not be enough for you to truly become an expert. You're probably reading this book in the comfort of your home, or perhaps by the pool-side on vacation. Neither of these environments is rich with other fund-raisers with experience. When I walk into a coffee shop looking for other people just like me, I'm usually the one who is out of place. I'm the weirdo. But when I attend a syndication conference, I'm in a room full of people who are "normal", just like me.

If your hobby is fly fishing, or quilt making there are endless numbers of clubs and groups locally and online to find like-minded people to learn from, build relationships with, and advance your skills. These communities of interest are essential for you to develop your skills.

Where do entrepreneurs looking for capital hang out? There are investment conferences around the country that specialize in some aspect of raising money. Here are a few that I recommend:

- Pitbull Conferences
- Family Office Conferences
- Real Estate Guys™ Seminars
- Masterminding with other entrepreneurs
- CEO-Space

Be careful. Many seminars are designed for rookies and are thinly veiled magnets for high pressure sales pitches for courses and coaching programs. These are not what you want. You want to attend conferences that have a high proportion of repeat attendees. They keep coming back for the expanded knowledge and for the first rate networking opportunities.

By far the most accessible people are those who attend conferences and have become successful as a result of collaboration with others. When I attend conferences, I often arrange my travel to arrive a day before the conference. I use that extra time to schedule one-on-one meetings with key people whom I'm building or maintaining relationship with. I also use the time outside the formal agenda to schedule as many meetings as possible. This includes breakfast meetings, lunch meetings, dinner meetings. Conference days are long and exhausting. They usually start at 7:00 AM and end late in the evening. The result of these meetings is usually an agreement to follow-up on something specific after the conference.

Super-stars in your environment

People who have achieved greatness in business are often surrounded by others who also achieve great success. This is a little bit like a solar system surrounded by planets and satellites. The planets don't shine like the star, but they have substantial mass in their own right. I personally know many successful people who have created significant success in part, as a result of being in an environment with other successful people.

One such star is Kevin Harrington. Kevin was the inventor of the infomercial genre. Over the years he has sold billions of dollars worth of products through his channels. He has been an active investor in numerous products. Some of the most visible have been on the acclaimed TV show "Shark Tank" where Kevin was one of the Sharks. Kevin is very visible as a star, but has also made a lot of people wealthy. In the shadow of Kevin Harrington is Dan Borislow. Dan is the inventor of the Magicjack digital phone product. Kevin was an early investor in the project. Dan didn't just need money. Money in many respects can be treated as a commodity. Dan needed Smart Money. Kevin's experience with bringing products to the mass market was critical to the success of the Magicjack. Dan ultimately went on to sell over $120 million dollars worth of MagicJack products (and counting), for the benefit of both Dan and Kevin.

I have been extremely blessed to build some amazing relationships by being in the right environment. The right environment will bring you:

- Ideas
- Opportunities

- Best practices
- Introductions
- Encouragement
- Money

Yes, some relationships will also result in capital for your projects. Most will not. I regularly build relationships with people who are similarly successful. The benefits of environment go far beyond capital.

Many of these relationships result in an ongoing process called a Mastermind. This concept was coined by Henry Ford and documented by Napoleon Hill in his famous book "Think and Grow Rich". A Mastermind occurs when a group of like-minded, but diverse people get together to analyze a problem together for the benefit of the stakeholder. The members of the Mastermind are not stakeholders in the outcome. The independence from the outcome is one of the benefits of the participation. Having no vested benefit in the outcome means that the advice and ideas are unbiased.

I regularly participate in Masterminds. For example, I host a monthly Mastermind with Mr. George Ross. George achieved celebrity status as Donald Trump's advisor on the TV show "The Apprentice". George is distinguished by a career spanning more than 60 years and has completed more real estate deals in New York City than perhaps anyone else alive today. Prior to working for Donald Trump, George worked for Goldman and DiLorenzo where he personally negotiated over 700 real estate transactions over a ten year period. George doesn't do business with me. He is not a stakeholder. He simply provides advice, wisdom and perspective like no other. I'm much richer for the opportunity to bounce ideas off him. This is all part of the business environment that I create for myself.

Some ideas are very simple, but have a profound impact on my business success. For example, I receive ideas on how to structure deals that provide better terms for my core team and for my funding partners.

Relationship building is a critical aspect of "environment". I make a point of scheduling multiple meetings every week, sometimes having lunch with other developers. These meetings have no fixed agenda. The premise is often as simple as "I'd like to get to know you better, and understand your goals. Perhaps there's some way I may be of help in the future." In order for that approach to be effective, they need to see me as someone they would willingly accept help from.

I track the results of these meetings in a software system. I write notes on the results of each meeting in the database. My staff will regularly review the database and suggest follow-up on a periodic basis. This kind of deliberate relationship management means that the my most important business relationships don't go stale. After all, it's these relationships that form the core of my eco-system, the environment.

Life as an Entrepreneur and Social Media

There are very strict rules around solicitation for investment. In most jurisdictions, solicitation is not permitted. There are a few select exceptions, and the rules must be adhered to very strictly. Unless you're fully prepared to be 100% in compliance with these rules, the safe bet is to never post anything online that could be construed as a solicitation. Never, ever, solicit in social media, or anywhere online unless you're 100% in compliance with the rules for your local or federal securities commission.

When I meet people in person, I make sure that I connect with them on social media. The most effective platforms for my purposes are FaceBook and LinkedIn. I only use these platforms to communicate excitement about day-to-day projects and various media exposure. I call this Buzz marketing. The only purpose is to share excitement about what I'm doing. I use social media to remain visible to my relationships in a way that is (hopefully) engaging story-telling. It's a fine line between engaging story-telling, and annoying self-promotion. By sharing some personal information I'm keeping the relationship warm so that the next time we speak in person, there is a context to the conversation. By being visible, I find that my associates tend to make more valuable introductions, more frequently, and in larger numbers. I can't say there is a direct mathematical relationship between my social media posts and introductions, butthe number and quality of introductions continues to rise.

Branding and Positioning

Building a strong environment also involves building a reputation and being visible in the community. I made a decision in 2012 to write my first book. The purpose of writing the book was to fill a void in the marketplace. However, it wasn't to make money from book sales. The purpose was to position me as an authority. With this positioning I could get more media exposure to further position me as an authority. This strategy was very effective. In 2013 I appeared on several radio shows in Toronto. On the basis of my appearance on these shows, a major developer in Toronto agreed to meet with me and we entered into a transaction negotiation. He said, "I heard you on the Real Estate Talk Show. You were saying the right things. That's why I agreed to meet with you." That transaction ultimately resulted in a strong revenue year in 2014. I can clearly trace the investment in positioning, branding and media exposure as a key element in achieving my financial goals in 2014.

I also choose to get involved in various real estate investment clubs. These clubs have a need for leaders to step forward and add value. These positions have a fancy title, but pay absolutely zero. By becoming involved, I have the opportunity to become known in the investment community. The person on stage clearly is better marketed than the person sitting in the back row of the room. Whenever I get the chance, I choose to be on stage. I'm not there to self-promote. That's too self-serving. Instead, by adding value, I get the benefit of visibility. That's a fair trade of value.

3 Because it's the Law

Before we dive into the technique for raising money, it's important to know that there are rules to follow. If you ignore these, you may find yourself facing a lawsuit, a securities fraud investigation, or perhaps a securities conviction complete with penalties and maybe an orange uniform.

In most jurisdictions there are strict rules governing securities. There are three types of securities:

1) Registered securities
2) Exempt securities
3) Illegal securities

Registered securities are of the type that you would find listed on a public stock exchange. In the US, the Securities and Exchange Commission at the federal level, along with state level bodies governs the rules around securities. In Canada, the securities commissions of each province govern the regulation of securities at the provincial level. Some of the smaller provinces don't have the scale to have fully developed regulations and in some cases have copied the rules of the Ontario Securities Commission or the British Columbia Securities Commission which are more established by virtue of having publicly traded stock exchanges in their jurisdiction. In this book, we're only going to reference US Securities and Exchange Commission regulations and Ontario Securities Commissions rules.

Note that securities law is one of the fastest moving areas of law. Even lawyers who practice in this area daily are often checking back to make sure they're current with legislative changes, policy changes, and new legal precedence. I repeat, please, please, please do not use this book as a source of legal advice. That's not the intention. The intent is to arm you with enough knowledge that you can ask your attorney intelligent questions. The securities law interpretation of any situation will be specific to that situation alone and may not translate to others that are similar.

What is a Security?

In the US, not all offerings of securities must be registered with the SEC. The most common exemptions from the registration requirements include:

- Private offerings to a limited number of persons or institutions;
- Offerings of limited size;
- Intrastate offerings;

So the first question is: "What is a security?"

Generally speaking, if there is an investment of monies with the expectation of a profit and the investment has a passive nature on the part of the investor, then it might be considered a security. If two partners get together and form an entity together to start a business, and both are actively involved in the day to day operation of the business, then it would NOT be considered a security.

However, if one of the partners is active, and the other is passive having invested only money, then it would be considered a security. Why is this important? Because securities are governed by securities laws.

Taken directly from the Act:

> Any note, stock, treasury stock, security future, bond, debenture, evidence of indebtedness, certificate of interest or participation in any profit sharing agreement, collateral-trust certificate, reorganization certificate or subscription, investment contract, certificate of deposit for a security, fractional undivided interest in oil, gas, or other mineral rights, any put, call, straddle, option, or privilege on any security, certificate of deposit, or group or index of securities (including any interest therein or based on the value thereof), or any put, call straddle, option, or privilege entered into on a national securities exchange relating to foreign currency, or, in general, any interest or instrument commonly known as a "security" or any certificate of interest or participation in, temporary or interim certificate for, receipt for, guarantee of, or warrant or right to subscribe, to or purchase any of the foregoing. 15 U.S.C 77b(a)(1).

Wow, that's extremely broad and sweeping.

This is important because the US government has established a much lower threshold for establishing securities fraud compared with common law fraud.

The precedent setting case was the now famous Supreme Court decision of the SEC vs Howey in 1946. In that case, the court held that land sales contracts for citrus groves in Florida, couple with warranty deeds for the land and a contract to service the land were "investment contracts" and thus "securities".

The essential feature of a security under the Securities Act and confirmed under Howey was whether a contract exists whereby a person invests his money with the expectation of a profit, solely from the efforts of the promoter or third party. According to the court, it's immaterial whether the interests are evidenced by formal certificates or by nominal interests in the assets employed by the entity.

So against this broad definition, chances are that if you're raising money to grow your business whether it's a loan or a share, you're into the world of securities.

It's important to note that each state has its own rules, and in Canada the rules are governed at the provincial level by each provinces security commission. We're just discussing general guidelines. This book is no substitute for legal advice.

Registered Securities

Registered securities go through an extensive process with the regulator to ensure the public is protected. This process involves the creation of a prospectus and filing the prospectus with both federal and state level regulators. These filings include:

- A description of the company's properties and business;
- A description of the security to be offered for sale;
- Information about the management of the company; and

- Financial statements certified by independent accountants.

After about a year and tens of thousands of dollars in legal and accounting costs you may get the right to sell a security. That seems like an onerous process, and it certainly carries a number of obligations.

Exempt Securities

So you might be asking whether a simple loan is a security. It depends. There are a number of exemptions for loans depending on who the lender is, and the term of the loan. For example, banks are exempt from securities laws for certain types of loans and bank deposit accounts. Loans between private individuals that are less than 9 months in duration can be considered commercial paper and are also exempt. In some jurisdictions a mortgage will exempt a loan from being considered a security. However, that isn't necessarily true in all cases.

There are numerous other exemptions. For the purpose of focus and clarity, we'll only dive into the ones that in our experience are the most relevant and cost effective.

Regulation D, rule 506

There are several exemptions under Regulation D. They are numbered rule 501, 503, 504, 505, 506. Each of these rules has different criteria. I believe the most useful rule is 506 and that is what we will discuss in this book. There are many other books and documents readily available that dive deeply into the other rules under Regulation D. Rule 506 can be further divided into 506(b) and

506(c).

Under 506, there is no limit to the amount of money that can be raised. The difference between the two is whether you can accept monies from accredited or non-accredited investors.

Accredited Investor

The SEC has a strict definition of an accredited investor. This definition changed in 2010 with the introduction of the Dodd Frank Act. Taken directly from the SEC investor bulletin is the definition of an accredited investor.

An accredited investor, in the context of a natural person, includes anyone who:

- Earned income that exceeded $200,000 (or $300,000 together with a spouse) in each of the prior two years, and reasonably expects the same for the current year, OR
- has a net worth over $1 million, either alone or together with a spouse (excluding the value of the person's primary residence).

On the income test, the person must satisfy the thresholds for the three years consistently either alone or with a spouse, and cannot, for example, satisfy one year based on individual income and the next two years based on joint income with a spouse. The only exception is if a person is married within this period, in which case the person may satisfy the threshold on the basis of joint income for the years during which the person was married and on the basis of individual income for the other years.

In addition, entities such as banks, partnerships, corporations, nonprofits and trusts may be accredited investors. Of the entities that would be considered accredited investors and depending on your circumstances, the following may be relevant to you:

- any trust, with total assets in excess of $5 million, not formed to specifically purchase the subject securities, whose purchase is directed by a sophisticated person, or
- any entity in which all of the equity owners are accredited investors.

In this context, a sophisticated person means the person must have, or the company or private fund offering the securities reasonably believes that this person has, sufficient knowledge and experience in financial and business matters to evaluate the merits and risks of the prospective investment.

Rule 506(b) and 506(c)

506(B)	506(C)
Unlimited raise	Unlimited raise
Up to 35 non-accredited investors permitted	Accredited Investors Only
Advertising is not permitted	Advertising allowed
Solicitation is not permitted	Solicitation allowed
Must have a pre-existing relationship with investor (friends and family)	No pre-existing relationship needed
No bad actors permitted as syndicators or more than 20% controlling ownership	No bad actors permitted as syndicators or more than 20% controlling ownership

No need to register with each state	No need to register with each state
Verification of suitability for investors can be done by "check the box"	Take Reasonable Steps to Verify Investors Accreditation

A Regulation D fund is one of the most effective tools for an entrepreneur. In the early days, these filings were expensive to put together. Legal fees generally ranged from $30,000-$70,000 to put this together. This is a bargain compared with a registered offering, but is still a steep hurdle to overcome when you're looking to raise funds.

Today, the vast majority of Regulation D funds are prepared using templates. The content of the document is still venture specific, but the template simplifies the preparation of the filing. There are many good quality templates available for purchase online for a modest cost. With the addition of some legal consulting, a full 506 filing can often be completed for less than $10,000.

In some cases, the proposed investment may appear to be in the gray zone. It looks like it may fall under one of the exemptions from being classified as a security, but against another definition could possibly be considered an investment contract (and therefore a security). In such a case, the additional complexity is that it may be exempt at the federal level, but not according to state regulations. The safe course of action is to complete a simple 506 filing and thereby reduce the risk of being outside of compliance. Furthermore, the 506 filing also exempts you from having to register with each individual state. A good securities attorney can keep you on the right side of the law for minimal cost.

Crowd Funding

One of the newest exemptions falls under a rule that was implemented in 2015 under the JOBS Act, or the so-called crowd funding rules. Like any piece of modern legislation, it is complex and spans 685 pages.

There are a number of benefits and limitations of this approach. There are two tiers of offerings possible under the new legislation.

Issuers of this type of Tier 2 offering are limited by the amount a non-accredited investor under Rule 501(a) of Regulation D can purchase to no more than: (a) 10% of the greater of annual income or net worth (for natural persons); or (b) 10% of the greater of annual revenue or net assets at fiscal yearend (for non-natural persons). In addition the investor is limited based on the past 12 month income and net worth history to:

(i) The greater of $2,000 or 5 percent of the lesser of the investor's annual income or net worth if either the investor's annual income or net worth is less than $100,000; or

(ii) 10 percent of the lesser of the investor's annual income or net worth, not to exceed an amount sold of $100,000, if both the investor's annual income and net worth are equal to or more than $100,000;

Benefits:
- You can advertise and solicit to non-accredited investors.

- You can conduct parallel raises, subject to rules and limitations
- Access to the broader marketplace and a nationwide audience

Drawbacks:
- You can raise no more than $1,000,000 in a 12 month period
- You must use a qualified intermediary - either an SEC broker/dealer or a newly created funding portal registered and regulated by the SEC.
- Severe restrictions on what you can disclose publicly outside the portals
- Investors can change their mind within 48 hours of the close of the raise.
- Large number of investors. You could have hundreds of investors, largely unsophisticated. The lack of sophistication means the possibility of misunderstanding goes way up.
- Disclosures. You must provide different levels of information, depending on the size of the raise. For raises over $500,000 you must provide the investors, the portal, and the SEC audited financial statements from an independent CPA.
- Progress updates including annual reports, a disclosure statement similar to the original offering
- Cost. The SEC estimates the costs associated with the portal between 4.1% and 11.7% depending on the fees and the size of the raise.

If you're looking to undertake larger projects where the $1,000,000 limitation is too low, you can combine a crowd funded campaign with a Regulation D, 506 fund as long as both are in full compliance.

There are very specific constraints around how you advertise under the crowd funding rules. You can advertise widely, provided your advertising name the intermediary being used, directs people to the intermediary's platform, contains information about the terms of the offering, and correctly names the issuer of the offering. The *terms of the offering*means the amount of securities offered, the nature of the securities, the price of the securities and the closing date of the offering period. Consult the SEC website for the most current interpretation of the rules around how to conduct a crowd funding.

Illegal Securities

It may seem strange to talk about this category - Illegal Securities. They're not mentioned to advocate in favor of breaking the law. But you need to be aware that many offerings in the marketplace are not in compliance with the law. Many of them are successful (investor doesn't lose money) and are never contested or even reported to the governing authorities. Illegal offerings are surprisingly common. The people offering these are generally doing so out of ignorance. As you know, ignorance isn't an excuse for breaking the law. Again, most of these are mis-steps where nobody is harmed.

However, there are few that unfortunately go bad. In these cases, the penalties can range from monetary, to criminal. The laws are particularly stringent around disclosure. The fact that a project may run into trouble isn't against the law, per se. The problem usually arises around filing and disclosure. When the risks are mis-represented, the burden shifts to those with the fiduciary responsibility. As I said before, these fall into the category of "securities fraud" for which the SEC has established a very low threshold. Simple failure to adequately disclose or file paperwork in a timely manner may constitute "fraud" under rules. You don't need to be a crook to commit fraud under these definitions.

As an entrepreneur looking to raise capital, you owe it to yourself to be aware of the rules. Why would you put yourself in the position of additional liability simply out of ignorance? It's possible that you may have already initiated some projects that are not in compliance. If so, what that really means is that you've effectively signed a personal guarantee on the funds, unless you want to run the risk of an SEC action being brought against you.

As an investor, you owe it to yourself to be aware of the rules. You can't naturally assume that the promoter of the project or opportunity is in compliance with the rules.

A few simple questions can get to the bottom of this:

1) Is what you're offering a security?
2) If not, why not?
3) If yes, under what exemption does the security fall?

I'm not saying that everything you do must be an exempt security. If there is a sufficient element of control, then the investment would not be considered a security. I repeat, the purpose of this book is NOT to provide legal advice. As always, consult your own qualified legal counsel who can provide advice and interpretation of the law, specific to your situation.

4 Relationships and Relational Capital

There are many types of capital in existence today. We will take a small detour into philosophy for a few minutes.

Financial capital can be found in your bank account, or on your personal or corporate balance sheet. When we talk about capital, people naturally think we're talking about money, but there are other forms of capital that are as valuable, and in some cases far more valuable than money.

Educational capital is representative of how much knowledge you possess. For example a PhD student can be said to have more educational capital then a high school graduate. By reading this book, you're hopefully increasing your educational capital. Educational capital by itself doesn't translate directly into a better project, a better business or a better life. It requires the knowledge to be put into action.

Physical capital can be used to represent your personal health. If you are not healthy or if you are sleep deprived you will not be able to perform at the level you hope will achieve your dreams and desires. Your body is the gift that our creator has given you for as long as you're here with us on earth. The ability to conduct business is inextricably connected to your physical health and fitness. The most successful senior executives, politicians, and world leaders have a strict exercise regimen. I simply ask myself, if the President of the United States can find the time to exercise daily, what's my excuse? Surely my problems aren't anywhere near the depth or complexity of those in the White House.

Emotional capital is your body's ability to process emotionally charged events. The more emotional capital you have, the more resilient you will be in the face of adversity. Stephen Covey coined the term "Emotional Bank Account". The context was different. In that scenario, he was describing making emotional deposits and withdrawals in interpersonal relations. The same applies to the intrapersonal emotional bank account that exists within you. You need to replenish it with mental relaxation, mindfulness, meditation,

Relational capital is a measure of the value of all of your relationships. This is your ability to leverage your business relationships into a revenue stream. For example, in 2013 I visited the home of Paul Baylor who had previously owned and sold a furniture manufacturing company. He was 70 years old at the time. He had retired about 5 years previously and after sitting at home in his lovely estate, he was getting bored. So at age 69, he decided to restart his furniture business from scratch. In that first year, he managed to grow to $25 million in revenue from a standing start. He knew how to run a factory, but that wasn't enough. He knew how to lead people, but that wasn't enough. He knew how to build a new factory, but that wasn't enough. None of those highly valuable skills would help him bring $25 million in new sales with a brand new business. It was the value of his relationships that enabled that kind of startup growth. He knew who to call to get the orders. That's the value of relational capital. It applies to most industries.

Most Federal, State and provincial securities commissions have strict rules around solicitation for investment. In general, It is illegal to solicit for investment. There are a few specific exemptions depending on the jurisdiction. We've discussed many of them in the chapter dealing with legal aspects.

So how do you create new relationships to expand your capital base if you're not allowed to solicit? It's pretty simple. You create new relationships "just because" it's good to have more relationships. A long way down the road, a subset of those relationships may be a good fit for you to do business with. In the meantime, just invest in relationship building. Relationship building can be managed as a process, similar to a sales funnel. Except the outcome at the end of the process isn't a sale, it's a relationship.

The most difficult part of building any marketing funnel is going from cold to warm. It's time consuming. People who don't know you are generally less likely to give a warm reception. Our modern lives are so inundated with solicitations, that the filters are up most of the time. As a matter of survival, we are programmed to reject solicitations. So you can expect a high rejection rate. With a well crafted approach you may get a positive response rate of 30%. Even with such a high response rate, you will still need to approach a large number of people. The key is to connect with people in a way that is genuine and compelling. Part of this is to position yourself as a leader, as someone they want to get to know. You need to demonstrate from the first interaction that you don't "want something" from them. Nobody wants to feel used. So don't do it. The focus needs to be on genuine relationship building.

Social media has changed the way that people connect and communicate. Social media has enabled anybody with a following (Facebook friends, LinkedIn connections, Twitter followers, etc) to market themselves to their followers. I know that sounds ugly. When you share information about you with people you know, that is a form of marketing. So then the question becomes, what do you want to share? Here are a few choices:

- Holiday photos
- Pictures of your cat (fun but not that helpful)
- Excitement about progress in a project
- Educational tips
- Events in your business life
- Commentary on trending topics that are relevant to your industry

It's all about positioning yourself in a way that your friends and followers will find engaging. I am a strong believer in marketing yourself in a way that doesn't feel like marketing. Buzz marketing is a way of sharing excitement about what you are doing. Story telling is a very powerful form of marketing. You want to position yourself exercising leadership. You want to show that you're generous, that helping others achieve greatness is part of your makeup.

Marketing requires seed planting, education, repetition, social proof and authenticity. That's it. Simple right?

Nobody likes to be sold. We are bombarded with images, sounds, logos, advertisements of all kinds. We filter out the vast majority of these. As I am sitting at my desk writing, I can scan my environment and count the number of advertisements they are hitting me right here in my home office. I count no less than 30 brand logos within my potential field of view. Unless I am looking for them, I don't even see them. There is the Apple logo on my phone, the Acer logo on my screen, the Fujitsu logo on my scanner, the HP logo on my printer. There is even a logo on my coffee cup. You get the idea.

There is so much that we simply can't cope. Our basic survival strategy is to prevent mental overload. We only allow a few select items to come into focus that we can reasonably process at a given point in time. The human mind is an amazing computer. But it can only keep a small number of items in its short term working memory. This number varies from one individual to the next. But for most people, the number is somewhere between 6-10 items. More than that causes mental overload.

So how to you prevent from being relegated to the overload category? You develop a relationship. Imagine the following scenario. Someone you don't know calls you on the phone and says:

> **"There's a great seminar coming up in two weeks that I think would be perfect for you. It's only $199."**

What is your reaction? For most people, it would result in a negative reaction. Who are you? Why are you trying to sell me something? What's the catch? How do you know it would be perfect for me? You don't even know me!

Now imagine if a close friend calls you up and says exactly the same thing.

"There's a great seminar coming up in two weeks that I think would be perfect for you. It's only $199."

What is your reaction now? Most people would say something like. "Tell me more". What's the difference? The words are exactly the same. The difference is one of context. In the first case, there is no relationship. So by default, the caller is put in the "delete" category along with all the other thousands of inputs that overload us. In the second case, the context is one of a friend offering something of potential value, from a perspective of generosity. You can never be seen as a person who solicits. You must develop a ratio of giving to asking that is so overwhelmingly biased toward giving that people won't even notice when you ask.

World renowned author Seth Godin describes this simply as "Giving". When you ask someone to register with their email address in order to get a free white paper, or a free e-book, you are conducting a transaction. A transaction assumes reciprocity. If I give you $10,000, and you give me a car in return, that is a transaction. It is considered a fair transaction if I got a good car at a fair price.

When you give, you are simply giving. There is no expectation of reciprocity. If you give often enough, then the rare time that you ask will not seem like you are asking. The ideal ratio of giving to asking is 20 to 1. As a minimum the ratio should be no less than 10 to 1.

In order for education to be authentic, it must be received as a gift, not a transaction.

Repetition is need to create memory. This is true for anything. You need to repeat at least three times for something to sink in. Something said once will be merely transient and quickly forgotten. Some speakers on stage will often repeat an impactful sentence for emphasis. Why do they do this? Any message that they want the audience to retain should be repeated. We are, after all, creatures of memory. When we conduct any physical movement, such as walking, we rely on muscle memory. That memory is created through repetition. The more the repetition, the more it becomes familiar, and second nature. Ideas operate the same way.

Relationship as a Foundation for Investing

Would you entrust millions of dollars of your hard earned money with someone you don't know? Most people would not. At the foundation of any business transaction is relationship. It must be real. It must be genuine. That is why the "friends and family" exemption exists in securities law in many jurisdictions. Relationship is foundational to establishing the second critical criteria "Trust". But we'll talk more about that later.

If the net worth of your 5 closest friends won't launch and sustain your business, you will need to develop new relationships in completely different circles. You will want to develop relationships with high net worth individuals who can make a significant impact on the capitalization of your business if they choose to at some point in the future.

Some people go out and "network". I don't like that term because it has a utilitarian feel to it. It's a form of using people to achieve a business goal. Nobody wants to be used. Relationships have to be genuine at their very foundation.

If you try to develop a relationship with an ultra high net worth individual, there is going to be an imbalance. You have to acknowledge it up front.

How do you develop relationships with high net worth individuals? This can be intimidating for many people.

> *"They'll never want to hang out with me. They have so much money and power. I have nothing to offer them."*

Sometimes (financially) rich people choose to hang out with other rich people simply because it's easier. Rich people understand the problems of rich people better than poor people do. Poor people can't relate. The wealthy man wants to talk about the latest discussions coming out of the World Economic Forum in Davos. Poor people are talking about the latest auditions for America's Got Talent. The two worlds simply don't intersect in a meaningful way.

A wealthy person isn't going to be interested in the latest features in a Ford Focus. They're going to be interested in the paddle shifting performance of the latest Ferrari. Again, they have a tough time relating to one another.

A wealthy person will talk about the quality of the latest vintage of Chateau Margaux and the futures forecast for the vintage. A poor person will talk about whether Yellow Label is on sale at the liquor store.

If you want to fit in and develop relationships with wealth, you need to figure out how to relate, even if wasn't part of your background. How do you do that? Start studying. Look at what rich people do, and start becoming familiar with it. Look at what poor people do and stop doing it.

When there is a large imbalance between the net worth of two people, it can seem like the person with less is interested in the relationship "because" the other person has more. That's not a healthy dynamic. It can lead very quickly to the person with money feeling used and abused. People with money are still people at the core. They want genuine relationships just like anybody else.

Relationships are based on common interests, on adding value to each other lives, and on shared values and outlook. I've managed to develop relationships with some amazing people. Throughout that time, I've never abused the relationship or asked them for something. I've always taken the perspective of giving. If you think about your best friends, ask yourself the question "Why are you friends?" You probably have some shared experiences, and shared values. You're can often finish each other's sentences. You're kindred spirits.

One of my great passions is sailing. I've developed some amazing lifelong friendships based on that shared passion. I've heard some people recommend that you "Fake it till you make it". That's the most ridiculous idea ever. I believe it's much better to approach each situation with honesty, confidence, and integrity. Simply act as if you belong.

Some high net worth people love to play golf. Unfortunately, that's not one of my interests. I'm terrible at golf. I could not genuinely develop a rapport with someone around golf because it wouldn't be honest. I don't love it, and it would be obvious in minutes to anyone who is truly passionate about golf. One of my mentors has a net worth of over $300 million and he loves golf. It's not something we talk about. We've found other things that interest us both, such as travel on cruise ships. We talk about philanthropy, travel, the economy, world events. We rarely talk about my business unless we're having a mentoring moment. It's extremely important not to put business ahead of the relationship.

A great way to relationship build with high net worth people is by sharing philanthropic interests. Rich people generally like to give back to the community and champion specific causes. For some, it might be a particular disease, it might be a social issue such as addiction. There are so many causes. In the United States there are over 68,000 charitable foundations alone. Behind many of these are high net worth families and individuals. A great place to develop these relationships is to attend charitable events. You don't need to be a billionaire to attend an event and develop a relationship around a common cause. You can contribute time, and work on projects for the charity. High net worth people tend to spill opportunities that most others will never see. There are only so many hours in the day. A wealthy person will only go after the ones that make sense for them. Their cast-offs will not be of interest to them, but they may be very interesting for you and I. I find that the inner circle of wealthy people also become wealthy. Funny how that happens. It's back to the often quoted parable "Who you hang out with is who you become".

5 Trust

Trust is at the foundation of every successful business relationship and personal relationship. There is a direct correlation between speed and trust. When strong trust exists, decisions get made too quickly. When trust is lacking, you can expect days and weeks of due diligence. The psychological contract of trust is complex and has multiple layers. At the root of this psychological process is the meaning that we as individuals attach to what we observe.

New York Times columnist Thomas Friedman writes in his book the world is flat, this new flat economy revolves around partnering and relationships. Partnering and relationships thrive or die based on trust. As Friedman says:

> *"Without trust, there is no open society, because there are not enough police to patrol every opening in an open society. Without trust, there can also be no flat world, because it is trust that allows us to take down walls, remove barriers, And eliminate friction at Borders. Trust is essential for a flat world..."*

Why is this important? In a flat world, it's possible to conduct business without barriers. Regulations don't get in the way. A small business can compete with big business and win. It allows the small to act with the credibility of big business, and it allows big business to compete with the speed and agility of a small business.

Trust is earned over time. It's not simply granted. Although some people are naturally more trusting than others. This is usually a function of how often and how deeply someone has experienced a breach of trust.

The astute funding partner wants to know:

- Can I trust you to ask the right questions about a project?
- Can I trust you to put together a good plan?
- Can I trust you to execute that plan?
- Can I trust you to evaluate and manage risk appropriately?
- Can I trust you to communicate in an open and transparent way?
- Can I trust you to communicate when there is a problem?
- Can I trust you with my money?
- Can I trust you to hire good people?

If the answer is "no" to any of these questions, then the funding relationship will run into difficulty.

You cannot assume that trust will be blindly granted. It must be earned.

A very common mismatch is one of speed. When a high level of trust exists, it is possible to move quickly. Some deals require fast execution in order to get them done. A highly disciplined investor will generally not cut corners in their due diligence. It will be very difficult to close a deal in four weeks that requires three weeks of due diligence before the investor is even convinced to make the investment.

The psychological contract of trust is rooted in knowing the other party well enough to know their motivation. If we see a behavior, it's human nature to attach meaning to that behavior.

Let's look at an example: if you're expecting someone to show up at a meeting and they show up 20 minutes late, it could mean any of a number of things - the meaning you attach to the other party's lateness is based on your level of trust. It could mean:

1) They're not trustworthy
2) They probably ran into traffic
3) They don't value me or my time
4) They had a personal emergency that delayed them

In reality, the choice of which meaning to attach to the situation is largely based on our own perception of the other individual. That perception might be grounded in fact, or fear, or fiction. Most of the time in the absence of information, human nature fills that void with something random. Humans hate a void. We don't know how to handle it.

As an entrepreneur, you have a responsibility to be aware of that information void. It's your job to fill the void with facts. Don't blame the other party for jumping to conclusions.

Trust Is a Two Way Street

Whether you're an entrepreneur looking for funding, or an investor looking to put money to work, trust is a two way street. The entrepreneur needs to trust the investor to deal with them fairly, and to ensure that the investor won't surprise them with unreasonable demands. It's a two-way street.

I'm sometimes asked by investors what the minimum investment is in a project. I generally prefer to work with sophisticated accredited investors because these people have more funds. More importantly, they're also generally less anxious about their investment because they've had more experience and can handle a little more risk without it affecting their quality of life.

I learned an important lesson about trust as a borrower. I once borrowed funds from an investor who only had $25,000 in cash. He wanted to put 100% of his cash into a single project. That was all the free cash he had in the world. All of our projects required much more funds, with the exception of a small land acquisition consisting of a single residential lot. So we agreed to put his money to work for a year at 12% interest, secured on title by a mortgage in first position. He turned out to be the most nervous investor I've ever experienced. After only a short time into the project, he would call frequently to find out the status. He was anxious about the repayment of funds. After six months, he called and said that his family wanted him to buy a property in South Asia and he needed his money back before our agreement had stipulated. This was completely unexpected at the time, but in retrospect, completely predictable. Within a few weeks we had managed to return his capital and recapitalize the project. Legally speaking, we had an agreement. I could have stuck to the letter of the agreement, but that would have been the wrong thing for the investor and ourselves. I learned a valuable lesson: I never want to tie-up too high a percentage of an investor's free cash in a single project. I also want to work with investors who are more sophisticated and have greater assets at their disposal.

When trust is present, you can count on the other party to behave in a consistent manner. When behavior that falls outside the expected pattern occurs, the knowledge of the underlying intentions makes it possible to maintain that trust.

By observing each of your relationships, you can draw conclusions about the level of trust that exists based on the nature of the interactions.

Low trust relationships are characterized by:

- Guarded communications
- Mistakes remembered and used as weapons
- Real issues not surfaced and dealt with effectively
- Energy draining and joyless interactions
- Evidence gathering of the other parties mistakes and weaknesses

If you are experiencing any of the above, chances are high that there is low trust somewhere in the relationship. You will need to engage in trust building activities before you can make effective forward progress in the relationship.

High trust relationships are characterized by:

- Uplifting and positive communication
- Mistakes are treated as learning opportunities
- Cooperative, close, vibrant relationships
- High collaboration
- Effortless transparent communication

Trust is a function of two main components: Character and Competence. Many people believe that trustworthiness is simply a matter of character. Is this an honest person? If you focus on this part alone, you're missing the other half. People need to know that you can deliver. It's not enough that you tried, and that you had good intentions. Did you deliver?

Trust building requires two parties to spend time together. The relationship is not tested by the good times, it's tested by how problems (which inevitably arise) are handled.

Stephen M.R. Covey describes the 4 core elements of trust in his book "The Speed of Trust". These are:

1) Integrity
2) Intent
3) Capability
4) Results

It's virtually impossible to draw conclusions on all four of these after just a couple of meetings. This is the result of traveling a path together. Trust is earned by sharing a journey together. This could be a journey in business, or a journey through adversity.

Start Small

As a trust building exercise, I will sometimes suggest that we start with a small project as a first project. Of course, what is small is in the eye of the beholder. For one person, a small project might be a $15,000 renovation, and for another it might be a 20 unit townhouse complex.

If this relationship is going to be critical to a future large venture or project, you may need a small project as a trust building exercise.

It's in the process of handling problems that you get to assess each of these four areas, integrity, intent, capability, and results. I have a few funding partners who I suggested we cultivate the relationship by starting small. Whenever I've done that, every single one has gone on to conduct repeat investments with me. Don't be desperate. Start small and value the personal relationship above the business relationship.

The Predatory Investor

There are a few investors and lenders out there who are intent on making you fail. These vultures will craft one-sided agreements that put them in the power position, and when even a minor stumble occurs will trigger a default clause. They're waiting at the sidelines rubbing their hands together, just waiting for the small trip-up. Their goal is to take over control of your venture and steal the equity and controlling interest from you for a small investment.

Unfortunately, there are lenders of this type out there. How do you recognize them? You need to perform due diligence on them as an entrepreneur. If this particular lender seems to have a high proportion of litigation in the portfolio, it may be a sign that they're a predatory lender. The only other explanation is that they're poor at conducting their own due diligence. Companies that are poor at due diligence don't survive very long. If they have a high default rate, and they're still in business, you probably have a vulture.

What are some common vulture tricks?

A hard money lender may offer to loan money at high interest rates, with high origination fees, a short term, and a low loan to value ratio. In such a scenario, the property is worth more to them in default than as a performing loan. Let's look at an example:

Loan Principal:	$250,000
Interest Rate:	12%
Origination Fees:	4%
Loan Term:	6 months
Renewal Terms:	2% renewal fee. Renewable upon written notice and payment of renewal fee, 60 days prior to the end of the term.
Loan amount cap:	Lesser of 70% loan to cost or 60% loan to value.
Market Value:	$500,000
Collateral:	First lien position, secured by mortgage.

Supplementary security:
- Personal Guarantee
- Assignment of Rents
- Confession of Judgment
- Deed of Trust

The loan is being used to flip a property. The first thing I note here is that the timeline for a project such as this is usually more than 6 months. Even if the renovation is small and can be completed in under 30 days, the time it will take to sell the property on the open market is outside the control of the property owner. This is often governed by the sales cycle, how long it takes to get a firm agreement of purchase and sale with full waiver of conditions. The borrower needs to renew the loan no later than 120 days into the loan. The likelihood is very high that they will need to renew before they know that the property will sell. If the property is scheduled to sell in the last 60 days, they still need to renew the loan, just in case the sale fails to close. If they fail to renew, they risk being in default if the loan extends past the 6 month term. The supplementary documents can put all the power in the hands of the lender. After all, they will argue, this is necessary to secure their investment. They hardly ever exercise these tools and only do so as a last resort they will tell you.

Let's look at two scenarios involving the above hard money loan:

Scenario 1:

Loan gets repaid in 5 months. Borrower pays 2% renewal fee "just in case".

Total paid to lender: $250,000 principal, plus interest and fees = $15,000 + $12,500 = $27,500 for 5 months which comes to an annualized effective rate of 26.4%. This is an expensive loan to be sure.

Scenario 2:

Loan is needed for more than 6 months. Borrower fails to renew. Triggers a default in month 6. The interest rate accelerates to 24% for every day past the due date.

Borrower owes interest and fees totaling $25,000 for the first 6 months. But the lender is going to foreclose due to the default. They will sell the property at fair market value of $500,000. In addition to getting their money back, they will make $25,000 in interest and fees, plus an additional $250,000 from the proceeds of the sale. They could make up to $275,000 in profit on a $250,000 loan.

There's a strong financial incentive for the borrower to fail. The lender can multiply their income by a factor of 11.

Now I know what you're thinking. Many states have judicial foreclosure rules or power of sale rules that ensure the lender only gets their principal and interest repaid. The excess is returned to the property owner. What I'm describing sounds far too pessimistic. If the lender has extracted a deed of trust and a "Confession of Judgment", then the borrower may have little recourse.

The most heavy-handed element is the "Confession of Judgment". This often buried as a clause in the mortgage, or the personal guarantee. It basically says that you waive your right to independent legal counsel and you give the lender the right to act on your behalf as legal counsel. In addition, you agree in advance to authorize that counsel to plead guilty on your behalf to any action brought against you by the lender in any court for any reason.

This is why you need to have a high degree of bilateral trust. It's not enough that the investor or lender trusts you. You need to trust the lender as well.

Imagine a scenario where the lender embeds a requirement for the borrower to send a bi-weekly status report. Failure to provide timely reports would constitute a default. The lender may be filling the agreements will all kinds of land-mines that are designed to trip up the unsuspecting borrower. One common clause is that a default by the borrower on any loan globally constitutes a default on this loan. Imagine if a borrower is 30 days late on a $5,000 credit card bill. They would technically be in default on the loan. The lender will ask for permission for them to check your credit. They will then check your credit multiple times during the term of the loan, and then call the loan as immediately due and payable.

Fortunately, none of these situations have happened to me. However, they are surprisingly common.

Not convinced yet? I personally know three lenders who are vultures. Don't be alarmed. They're not my friends. I just know who they are and I steer clear of them.

How to Establish Trust with an Investor?

The most important thing is to get a set of legal agreements that protect all parties, are fair to all parties, and is reflective of the intent of the agreement between the parties.

Good agreements consist of a balance between rights and responsibilities on both sides. Before drafting legal agreements, it's important to get alignment on the major terms of the agreement. This is done typically in point form on a one or two page term sheet. The purpose of the term sheet is to surface all the important terms that are of importance to both sides.

Banks are notorious for creating one-sided agreements. These put the lender in the power position. The terms of the loan, mortgage, assignment of rents, sworn statement of construction, personal guarantee can represent hundreds of pages of legal agreements. I read every word.

Some banks have a reputation of having a high rate of foreclosure. Others, have a very low default rate. That's a function of several factors.

1) How aggressive is the lender?
2) How strong is the bank's balance sheet
3) How good a job has the bank done in qualifying borrowers in general?
4) Is the lender overly exposed in a single class of asset?
5) Are the loans insured? If so, they will follow the more stringent underwriting criteria of the insurer.

Sometimes, the bank regulator will require a bank to strengthen their balance sheet and deal with some non-performing loans. This is designed to improve the solvency of the bank. The stress test results of the banks are a matter of public record and are published by the bank regulator. You might take the attitude that the lender is lending you money. You're not putting your own funds in the bank. In reality, the lender will often require you open a bank account with them. They will escrow funds for contingency, interest reserves, and credit enhancement. It's worth knowing that the bank is strong and not relying solely on your own deposits to fund the loan.

How is this possible? Let's imagine that the bank's leverage is 10x. This means that for every dollar in deposits, the bank can lend out ten dollars. Now imagine that you're asking for a $1M dollar loan. The bank asks you to deposit $100,000, or 8% of the total project value of $1,250,000. Based on your deposit of $100,000, the bank now has the ability to loan $1M against that deposit. You've funded your own loan to the bank!

6 Results

This final element of the trust equation is so important that it merits its own chapter.

What results can you show? Show me a track record of success. Show me what you've done, mistakes and all. Past results can often be a predictor of future results, but not always. Will you invest with someone who has lost money on eight out of their last ten projects? I wouldn't!

When people and businesses market themselves they tend to put their best foot forward. That's natural. Sometimes they only show the good stuff, and actually lie about the bad stuff. They lie by omission, or even worse, falsify the past or pretend it didn't happen. In a world where the former chairman of the NASDAQ, Bernie Madoff cheated thousands of investors out of billions of dollars, it's hard to perform thorough due diligence on everyone you meet. The scope and sophistication of his deception fooled many savvy investors. We're not assuming that everyone out there is a cheat. The majority of failures are not the result of deception, but lack of competence, honest mistakes. These translate into results.

Our American business culture relies heavily on past performance as an indicator of future results and rightly so.

Many businesses such as E-Bay and AirBNB use a rating system that enables customers to choose their seller based on their rating. This rating documents their track record. Reputation in business is part of that all-important foundation of trust. Social proof is harder to manipulate than a simple marketing brochure. So you're probably thinking, I'm starting out, I don't have a lot of results to point to. Some new investors see a dilemma in what I'm proposing. "How can I raise capital without a track record? How can I develop a track record if I can't raise any capital?" My response to that is simple. First of all, investors prefer to invest in businesses, not the self-employed. Business is a team sport. If you're not part of an investment business and you're just starting, then join an established business with a track record of success. Work in that business for a period of time. You can then legitimately borrow some of their credibility and track record.

A successful business requires diverse complementary skills in at least seven distinct areas. There is no way a single individual can span all of those skills. Even if they could there wouldn't be enough hours in the day to multi-task between all those different roles. The business would be limited to a very small size.

The seven areas are:

- Executive Leadership
- Financial Controls
- Technical Operations
- Quality Assurance
- Communicating with existing customers

- Communicating with prospective customers
- Internal Policy and Systems

Each of these seven areas requires a different skill-set. You may be one of the leaders of the organization, but not necessarily the expert at raising capital. There should be one or two key people in the organization who are tasked with developing the relationships and raising the capital. The track record you're representing isn't just your own, it's all the key members of the team. It's the collective track record.

It's inevitable that you will be better at some things than others. Probably the biggest mistake you can make is to play the lead role in too many disciplines. You simply don't have the skills. Each role has a different flow, and requires a different skill set. For example, it may be tempting to have the same person in charge of Technical Operations, and Quality Assurance. The same person can develop the knowledge and skill to perform both of these functions. However, the objectives of these two functions are fundamentally at odds with one another. Technical Operations is motivated and rewarded by delivery of finished product to the customer. Quality Assurance is interested in protecting the interests of the customer, even if it means a short term delay in delivery, or a reduction in profitability. There is an inherent conflict between these two roles and they must be managed independently.

Every business needs these 7 areas to be successful. Not only that, the successful business is focused on getting the right people in the right roles. I've witnessed many pitches from startup companies. All too often, there are members of the leadership team who are part of the team because they're friends with the CEO. That simply demonstrates poor judgment on the part of the CEO. It signals that the CEO isn't capable of recruiting the right talent, and that they're willing to compromise on business principles for non-business reasons. No investor wants to see those types of mistakes being made and putting investor funds at risk as a result.

In some cases, the CEO or some key team members simply are too inexperienced to instill confidence in the investors. Investors want to see results. They want to see depth and resilience in the team. They know that business is difficult. They know that unexpected problems will occur. The depth and resilience of the team is critical to ensure the safety of investors' money.

Metrics

If you're going to show results, you need to focus on business metrics that are meaningful measures of business performance. Investors want to see that you know how to properly instrument your business, collect the numbers, and make good business decisions with those numbers. There are so many business metrics, and some are more important than others.

1) Revenue
2) Profit
3) Cash Flow
4) Customer Satisfaction
5) Employee Satisfaction
6) Cash reserves
7) Return on Equity
8) Performance to schedule
9) Performance to budget.
10) New customer
11) Client lifetime value
12) Customer conversion rate
13) New Customer acquisition rate
14) Customer attrition rate
15) Employee attrition rate

16) New Customer Leads
17) Book to Bill Ratio
18) Cash reserves
19) Cash burn rate

You'll want to lead with the financial metrics Investors interest may be broad, but they're primarily interested in the financial performance of the organization. Of all these metrics, the most important is cash-flow. It determines the financial health of the organization from which many of the other financial metrics can be derived.

7 Compelling Opportunity

Many entrepreneurs and real estate investors are generally too "deal focused". They put all their energy into the deal. It's all about the deal. Hopefully by now, I've convinced you that there are so many other factors that cannot be neglected. Once you've got all those other factors under control, you also need to have a good deal, or as I prefer to call it, a compelling opportunity.

A compelling opportunity is somewhat in the eye of the beholder. I have heard so many times the sentence, "I had a great deal, but I could not get it funded." In my experience, all good deals get done. Not only that, they get done quickly. The only question is: "Will it be you, or me, or the next guy?"

The most sophisticated and savvy investors have a specific model that they pursue. It may be a specific category of asset. For example, medical office buildings, self storage, residential apartment buildings, or retail storefronts. Someone who specializes in medical office buildings is very unlikely to jump on a great deal in industrial space. They simply will not understand that business well enough to see the opportunity as compelling.

In my world, I only look at opportunities that can generate at least

30% net profit within the initial 12 months of the project. I see other investors pursuing opportunities that will generate 15% or perhaps 20% net profit margin. I consider such margins to be far too thin, And represent too high a risk.

New Construction Sporting Facility

Some entrepreneurs try to get projects funded that are totally ridiculous. One investor approached me recently to build a new 85,000 square foot commercial building to house mixed use sporting facilities and retail concessions. The premise of the project was a 8% capitalization rate and the total cost of the project was estimated at $20 million dollars. This means that the project must generate $1.6M in net income annually. Let review the math...

Cap Rate = Net income divided by Total Investment

Therefore

Total Investment x Cap Rate = Net Income

$20,000,000 x 8% = $1,600,000

The investor said that the leases would be competitive at $11 per square foot. I did a simple calculation and divided $1.6M in net income by 85,000 square feet to give us the net rent per square foot. From this I deduced that the project would need to generate $18 per square foot to be viable, not the $11 per square foot he was quoting prospective tenants.

The developer was having a hard time getting the project funded. It's easy to see why. He would need rents that are 63% above the market for the project to be viable. No bank, or funding partner with any financial sense would ever fund this project under those terms. Some entrepreneurs simply are not good at analyzing their business in a simple, clear and objective way.

Skylands Park

By contrast, my partner and I had the opportunity to purchase a baseball stadium about one hour outside New York City. The stadium was originally built in 1993 at a cost of $11 million. It consists of 28 acres of land, 46,000 square feet of buildings, parking for 2,000 cars, and a stadium with 4,200 seats with 18 luxury boxes. It included several commercial kitchens, a restaurant and bar which were vacant, but still had all the equipment. One building housed 8 batting cages with fully functioning ball launchers. The park used to be the home of the New Jersey Cardinals, one of the farm teams for the NY Yankees. Later, it was home to the Sussex Skyhawks. The stadium had set minor league attendance records in the past. It clearly had potential. The stadium was owned by a husband and wife. The husband died in 2011. They lost their team franchise. The wife was left holding an asset that was bleeding cash. She knew nothing about baseball. All she wanted was to move to Florida to be close to her children.

The park had minimal revenue. A daycare center was renting one of the buildings and bringing about $50,000 a year in revenue. The taxes, insurance and waste management contract were costing over $150,000 per year. The maintenance of the grass was another huge expense. The property also had a cell tower on the property with revenue from Sprint, Verizon and T-Mobile. The rent from the cell tower totaled $50,000 per year for the three carriers.

Again, the owner knew nothing about baseball, and knew nothing about how to sell a stadium. She listed it on Loopnet with a realtor who simply waited for the offers to pour in. The asking price was a little over $2 million. After several month they received a cash offer of $1.5 million which they declined. They later received a financed offer at $1.8 million which they accepted. The financing fell through and the stadium ended up on the market again. Nearly two years had passed since the original decision to list the stadium.

My partner and I decided that the break-up value of the stadium was greater than the purchase price. So we decided to offer $950,000 cash. Our offer was accepted.

The cell tower could be severed from the property and sold as a distinct asset. These are generally valued in the marketplace at a 7% cap rate. So based on the $50,000 per year in rental income, the tower would be worth approximately $700,000 on the open market as an income producing asset. There is an entire industry dedicated to the buying and selling of cell tower assets.

Cap Rate = Net income divided by Total Investment

Therefore

Net Income divided by Cap Rate = Resale Value

$50,000 divided by 7% = $714,000

By doing this, we could sell the cell tower for approximately $700,000 and lower our cost base on the remaining 28 acres, 46,000 square feet of buildings, and the stadium to only $250,000. This seemed like a compelling opportunity.

You don't need to be a financing genius to see the value in this opportunity. So we locked up the property in a purchase contract. We simultaneously found a buyer for the cell tower. We immediately started looking for people in baseball who might be interested in owning a stadium for a bargain price. We looked for league owners who were looking to expand. We looked for retired pro baseball players who might want to have a training camp facility. We even considered turning the parking into a drive-in movie theatre. After a few weeks we found an owner who had a stadium near Philadelphia. He was trying to start a new league, but would need 8 stadiums in total. Until he was sure he could secure 8 stadiums, he wasn't willing to commit to buying ours. So we offered him the right of first refusal if he loaned us the $250,000 needed to buy the stadium. He had secured his $250,000 with a mortgage in case we defaulted. We agreed on an 8% interest rate. For the cost of 8% of $250,000 we bought a stadium. Our upfront cash commitment was only $20,000. Any monkey could get the project funded at that point. This deal was easy to get funded. It was easy to get funded quickly. Once the opportunity became visible to people with the right perspective, it was easy.

To complete the story, my partner signed up a college team to rent the stadium for 13 games. The college brought in several truckloads of clay to re-level the diamond. It wasn't laser leveled in the way a major league stadium would require, but it was good enough. We held the stadium for about six month during which time we received an offer to purchase it for $800,000. We incurred about $80,000 in holding costs during the 6 month period. The net profit on the stadium was approximately $500,000.

Now you're probably thinking, how many distressed stadiums are there? Give me a real world example, not just a home run (forgive the pun).

My Signature Project

I believe in value creation. Sure home runs are great. I'll take them when they come along. The baseball team that only swings for the fences will lose every game. You need single base hits, doubles, triples, and home runs. Let's look at a base hit.

The "base single" project for me is a brand new 9-12 unit apartment building. These are comprised of small land assemblies consisting of anywhere from 3-6 infill lots in a dense urban setting. The location of these new construction projects is vitally important. They should be located on the edge of an expensive neighborhood on the fringe of the downtown core of a major city. Every major city in America has a band of real estate just outside the downtown core that has been neglected for 30 years or more. There is another major trend underway in most major cities in the US and Canada. As baby boomers are getting older, they're selling the 4 bedroom house with the picket fence in the suburbs and moving into town. They want a smaller townhouse in a trendy area with local restaurants, coffee shops, art galleries. All of it within walking distance. These areas are hot real estate markets. The march of progress in these areas is clearly visible. You can transition from a hot neighborhood to a rough area in the span of 1 city block. Our strategy is simply to purchase enough land on the "wrong" side of the street at a deep discount to the market. By building enough new product, the marketplace recognizes that the dividing line between the great neighborhood and the rough neighborhood has moved. We call this strategy "Buy on the line. Move the line." The dividing line is now located on the far side of my property. We repeat the strategy for a second time, a third time, as many times as market demand supports the march of progress. If you only build a single property, nobody cares, nobody notices. The value of your property will be largely determined by the surrounding properties. But if you build five or ten or twenty, the marketplace says "Oh, the line has moved". You can borrow the valuation from the expensive neighborhood next door rather than the rough area. This strategy delivers instant value creation.

I have several goals in a project like this.

1) Have a clear exit strategy within 1-2 years' time horizon.
2) Be able to return capital to investors in less than 2 years.
3) Create 30% net "profit margin" within 2 years without market appreciation.
4) Create positive cash flow during the construction phase, and over the life of the project.
5) Have a safe investment for our funding partners that does not put their capital at risk.
6) Generate long term cash flow beyond the 2 year time horizon.
7) Have a vehicle for long term capital appreciation.

By understanding the market value of the completed product, we can often ensure that our maximum investment will be no more than 70% of the appraised value of the completed building. If we can satisfy this criterion, then it's possible to refinance the project upon lease-up at, say, 70% or 75% loan to value ratio. This leaves us with 25%-30% equity and allows us to recapture 100% of our initial investment in the project. After the refinance, we have an asset that is generating positive cash flow for the long term, paying down the debt over the amortization period of the permanent financing.

A project such as this can take as little as a year, and more often takes two years. The majority of the time is consumed getting the required zoning approvals, site plan approvals, and building permits. This example is a 10 unit building located at 1228 N 25th Street in Philadelphia. The land was purchased for a total of $45,000. The structures on the land were demolished, and we sought a zoning variance to increase the allowed density from 8 units permitted by right, to 10 units. The total cost of the project including the land, construction, soft costs which include taxes, insurance, architectural was $1.05M. The completed building appraised for $1.8M. Upon completion and lease up we refinanced the building at 75% loan to value which yielded $1.3M. We managed to return 100% of the capital that we borrowed from our investors, plus an additional $150,000 which we invested in other projects. We were left holding an asset that is producing positive cash flow with zero cash tied up in the investment and a 75%/25% debt to equity ratio.

Business Opportunity

The first few examples have been real estate related. But there are a number of business opportunities that are equally compelling.

The key is to understand where the value lies. I've been involved in many startup companies over the years. Startups are difficult. Their chances of success are alarmingly low.

One in ten startup businesses achieves profitability. The 10% that achieve profitability will take five-seven years to become profitable. If your goal is to make money, go to Vegas. Your odds are better.

Most startups begin from a blank page with an idea to transform an industry. They have no revenue, no customers, just an idea. Most of them fail somewhere between startup and profitability because they don't have the resilience to withstand mistakes. Established businesses make mistakes all the time, but usually these are not fatal. They have the revenue, scale, customer loyalty and momentum to survive these missteps.

If you truly have a game changing idea, then go find an established adjacent business. It could be a potential partner, or customer with revenue. Acquire that business. Use the revenue stream from that newly acquired business to fund your startup. Its not a startup anymore. It's a business turnaround. It's a startup with a different starting point.

Raising capital to buy an existing business is much easier than a startup. It is easier to get 200 million for an existing business than 5 million to fund an idea. I show business leaders and entrepreneurs how to find the right business to buy, how to fund it, and how to execute the startup as an extension of the established business.

There is nothing wrong with starting new businesses. I will show you convincingly that the problem is the starting point. Starting on the ground floor is statistically doomed to failure. Starting on a mezzanine level is the path to success. By using this approach the chances of success have improved by 800%. The path to profitability has been accelerated by 5 years. Why would anyone build a business any other way?

8 Alignment

Investing is like a pair of shoes. You go to the store and you see a lovely pair of shoes. They're the most magnificent shoes. They're the shoes you've been waiting for all your life. You can hardly believe your luck, they're on sale this week. You give the salesperson your shoe size. They bring out the clean white box. Upon open the box you unfold the crisp tissue paper and place the shoe in position to try it on. If the shoe doesn't fit, it doesn't matter how lovely the shoe it, how great the sale price, you simply won't buy it.

When we describe the shoe metaphor it's easy to instantly understand. Nobody gets offended. Why is it that when we talk about money, the conversation gets awkward? I believe that the reason is that people have emotional baggage when it comes to money. Just like the pair of shoes, money has to fit the project. It seems strange because money seems so elastic. You can have more of it or less, use it for longer or shorter periods of time. It's not that money is the problem, it's the goals associated with money in the hands of the investor.

When you are raising capital you must ensure that there is perfect alignment between the goals for the project and the goals for the money. Money always has an agenda. If the goals for the money don't match your goals, don't take the money. This may sound obvious, But in practice it is easy to get emotionally wrapped up in the idea of getting the capital you need for a project. When emotions get in the way, bad things happen. If the lender needs the money back in 6 months, and your project needs it for 24 months, don't take the money. It might be tempting to get the project started, but you'll have heaps of trouble when the investor needs their funds back.

If you're looking to raise money, you should try to get into the mindset of the investor to better understand the investment criteria from the perspective of the investor.

Alignment breaks down into nine distinct categories. Briefly, the nine categories are:

1) Size of the investment.
2) Timing of the investment.
3) Term of the investment.
4) Annualized rate of return.
5) What is the risk?
6) What is the security?
7) What is the exit strategy?
8) What are the tax consequences?
9) What is the control structure?

The most sophisticated and savvy investors have well defined criteria for all of these elements. It's not enough to have a match on seven out of nine or eight out of nine. You have to fit perfectly on all nine. If not, don't take the money, and the investor should not make the investment.

Unsophisticated investors may have less defined criteria in some of these areas and it may be easier to get a fit. That's simply the result of inexperience. As time goes on and they gain experience they will become more sensitized to the right choices for themselves in each of the nine criteria. Don't accept inexperience as a substitute for fit. You may be setting yourself up for a surprise down the road.

We will now go into these categories in more detail.

Size of Investment

Investors have an ideal or target range for the size of deals that they do. Small investors with $500,000 to invest may want to make a series of investments of $75,000-$100,000 at a time. Ultra High Net Worth (UNHW) investors with hundreds of millions to invest may only consider projects above $50,000,000. They have tons of money, but won't consider an investment of $1,000,000. It's too small to be worth the effort of completing the paperwork. Sizing the investment is one of the most often discussed elements with funding partners. Regardless of the wealth of an investor, there are generally some factors that come into play for everyone. The decision of how much to invest on the part of the investor is a combination of several factors:

1) What percentage of my portfolio does this represent?
1) What percentage of my liquid cash will this consume?
2) What else might I need the cash for in the next while?
3) What opportunities will I miss as a result of tying up this cash?

Timing of the investment

When you're looking to raise funds, you must be extremely aware of the timing component. Raising money does take time. You should not be starting the conversation if you need the money by Friday. It's way too late. The more urgent the need for funds, the more desperate you will appear. Investors are not attracted to desperation. They are highly repulsed by it. They will run the other way.

You may be speaking with an investor today who may have funds available now, but has other business priorities that prevent them from actually taking the time to evaluate the investment in depth until a later time.

Raising of capital is not a continual activity. You might feel like you should always be on the lookout for money. In fact, this would be a mistake. Capital raising should take place over a finite time period. It might be 60 days, or 90 days for a given project. If the capital raise takes too long you run the risk that some capital commitments you received early in the process start to evaporate. There needs to be a defined start and end to the capital raise process.

Term of the Investment

How long will the cash be tied up? Investors have differing goals for the length of time they are willing to tie up their cash. This can be a function of a number of factors. If the funds are slated for use in retirement, then the time between now and retirement will be a factor. If the investor is in their 30's, they may be much more willing to undertake a long term investment than if the investor is in their 70's. Sometimes the investor has another plan for the cash in the future, but is willing to put the money to work in the meantime. There is no one right answer.

I had a learning experience with an investor who made a commitment to loan funds for a land acquisition for a one year term. After six months he approached me and said that his family wanted the funds to buy a piece of property in South Asia. Here was a case of a mismatch between the needs for the project and the needs of the investor. I could have chosen to hi-light the terms of the agreement to the investor and keep the money for the full term of the loan. In the end, I decided that it was a small amount of money. I could easily replace his funds and it didn't make sense to hold the investor's funds prisoner to the project. I found a way to return his capital within about 30 days.

In the wake of that repayment of capital, I asked myself what I had learned from the experience?

Had I really understood what his goals were? He was an unsophisticated investor who focused primarily on the rate of return as his most important factor in making the decision to invest. He hadn't been clear on his own investment horizon, and we failed to get clarity. I could take the position that he read the contract and he signed it knowing what he was signing. At the end of the day, would that really help?

Recycled Money

Some lenders have a relatively short term outlook on the recirculation of capital. This is because the return is divided into two components. The interest is paid out to the investors in the investment corporation. The originator of the loan who also services the loan (collects the interest payments) makes their money on the origination fee that is charged on the inception of the loan. If the term of the loan is too long, there is no way for the originator to get paid. They make their money on originations, not on the interest. So they want to put out the money on a regular basis. Sometimes a lender will specify a short term and then charge a renewal fee that is similar to the origination fee.

Rate of Return

Rate of return is an important factor, but often misunderstood. Sophisticated investors have a target for each element of their portfolio. Savvy money managers often divide their portfolio into three buckets:

1) Safety
2) Growth
3) Dream

This is called asset allocation. The expected rate of return in each bucket may be quite different, even for the same investor. Naturally the risk profile in each bucket will also differ. Why would an investor put cash in US Treasury bills earning less than 1%, versus a corporate bond that earns 5%, versus a high yield bond that earns 15%? The same investor may have money in all three types of investments simultaneously. Money in the safety bucket will be in low risk, low return investments. Money in the dream bucket may have a much higher risk tolerance. There is a correlation between rate of return and risk tolerance. That isn't to say that high risk investments will necessarily bring a higher rate of return. It's quite the opposite. The investor who is seeking the higher rate of return must evaluate what will naturally be a higher risk scenario. More to be said on this aspect later in this chapter.

How to Measure Rate of Return

The rate of return calculation can be complex. For simple cases, the math can be fairly straightforward. Let's look at a sample case:

A developer borrows $100,000. At the end of one year the lender is repaid the principal in full along with $10,000 in interest.

Principal:	$100,000
Interest rate:	10% fixed
Term:	One year
Payment terms:	At the end of 1 year

The rate of return quite simply is 10% on an annualized basis.

There are, however, many different types of deal structures. One of the most powerful financing vehicles is the convertible debenture. Cause this type of instrument starts out looking like a loan product, and then converts to an equity position like a share. While the loan is in place, the rate of return can be calculated in the same way as our simple case about. However, when the loan is repaid, any additional monies paid to the Investor represents an infinite return because of the initial investment capital has been returned.

Mathematically, this is incorrect. The proper way to calculate the rate of return is to treat the subsequent returns as part of the overall stream of cash flows. The internal rate of return calculation can it be used here.

I am not going to give a full math lesson here. Instead, let's look at how to use the IRR function in Microsoft Excel. The IRR function can be used to calculate the internal rate of return for any stream of periodic cash flows.

The example below is for a $100,000 investment that is repaid after one year with an additional $5,000 in interest. In this simple example, the business continues to generate cash flow of $5,000 a year as pure profit. This isn't interest, because the initial capital has been repaid. At the end of the 15th year, there is a lump sum payment, presumably the result of selling an asset. It's pretty obvious that calculating this rate of return is much more complex. Moreover, the rate of return changes over time, and it changes retroactively with each additional inflow of profit.

Year	Cash Flow	IRR
1	-$100,000.00	
2	$105,000.00	5%
3	$5,000.00	10%
4	$5,000.00	13%
5	$5,000.00	16%
6	$5,000.00	18%
7	$5,000.00	20%
8	$5,000.00	21%
9	$5,000.00	22%
10	$5,000.00	23%
11	$5,000.00	23%
12	$5,000.00	24%
13	$5,000.00	24%
14	$5,000.00	24%
15	$50,000.00	26%

The formula for calculating IRR in year 2 is "=IRR(B2:B3)". The calculation for year 14 is "=IRR(B2:B15)". You get the idea. This math isn't easy, but tools like Excel make it relatively straightforward to calculate, even if you aren't ready to go through the detailed calculations.

Security

The security in an investment is usually a piece of collateral that an investor can use to back up with their investment. One of the most common security instruments is a property mortgage. The level of security is a function of the loan to value ratio between the investment and the piece of collateral. Security and risk together can be combined to define safety. An investment with a 10% loan to value ratio and a high likelihood of default may still be a very safe investment. The likelihood is extremely high that the investor we'll be able to use the 90% equity in the collateral to recoup their 10% loan. On the other hand, an investment at 90% loan to value ratio with a low risk of default maybe considerably less safe.

There are many different types of security that can be employed to secure an investors monies.

Senior Debt
The senior debt is the mortgage holder who gets paid out first. The mortgage instrument is the legal document that the land owner gives to the lender as a security instrument. Years ago prior to our electronic records, deeds and mortgages were recorded at the County recorder office, Or the land registry office depending on the jurisdiction. The first person to record mortgage was said to be in

first position. It was literally a race to the record book. The second person to record a mortgage is in second position, and gets paid out second after the mortgage holder in first position is fully discharged.

Mezzanine Debt

Mezzanine debt falls between senior debt and equity. It is so-called because it occupies that middle layer. Many projects are completed with no mezzanine funding. But increasingly, mezzanine funds are used to reduce the amount of equity dollars (which are unsecured by definition) required to undertake the venture. Equity dollars are the scarce resource in most cases. The security of mezzanine monies is less than that of senior debt, because senior debt always gets paid first in the event of a default. Anything left after the senior debt is paid goes to the creditors in second position, then third position, and the finally the unsecured creditors if anything is left over after the secured creditors are paid. Naturally, the mezzanine lender will want a higher rate of interest to compensate them for the less secure position.

Cross-collateral.

In some cases, a lender isn't willing to loan against an unsecured asset, or where they believe their security to be weak. In that case, they may ask to encumber another asset that acts as additional collateral. These assets might be another piece of real estate that isn't encumbered.

Risk

Risk is one of the most misunderstood aspects. There is an entire science of understanding risk and quantifying it. Here is a deep dive on how to look at risk.

Let's define a few technical terms before we dive in. What is a risk?

Risk is anything that is not part of the plan.

Bad things can happen in any project. The presence or absence of a bad consequence is never the issue. The question is whether you have taken it into account. Let's imagine that your project might experience a weather related delay. It might be a snow storm, or perhaps a hurricane, depending on where you live. Weather delays happen. It's only a risk if your plan did not include weather delays as part of the plan. If you budgeted 7 days for weather delay in the plan, and you only experience 7 days or less delay, then there is no problem. The remaining risk is whether you will experience weather related delays in excess of 7 days.

Saying "High Risk" is ridiculous

When we talk about risk, we further subdivide risk into likelihood and impact. To say something is high risk is too superficial to be useful. A risk that has a high likelihood of occurrence, but a small impact may be completely acceptable. On the other hand, a risk with medium likelihood of occurrence and high impact may be completely unacceptable.

When I undertake a new project, I always put together a risk management plan. As an investor you should be asking any entrepreneur who you are considering investing with for their risk management plan. A proper risk management plan enumerates all of the risks in a project. They are further categorized according to the type of risk it represents.

Risk Types:
- Feasibility
- Time Delay
- One time financial cost
- Recurring financial cost
- Quality

Risks are qualified in terms of the type of risk they represent, and then they are quantified in terms of the scope of impact.

Feasibility risks are the most dangerous ones. This is a binary success or fail type of risk. There is no middle ground. The impact of a feasibility risk is always extremely high. It represents the complete failure of a venture.

Time-based risks can have varying degrees of impact depending on the amount of delay, and whether any critical dates are involved. We can often quantify the financial impact of a time based risk. The retailer that misses the Christmas sales season in the 4th quarter will lose more than a few weeks of revenue. They will miss an entire year worth of profit. Let's look at a concrete example:

New Construction Student Housing

A friend of mine recently completed a student housing project. If he missed the summer rental season for the upcoming school year, he would have lost an entire year worth of income not just a few days of income. He was in serious jeopardy of not being ready in time for the start of the academic school year. He was running one to two weeks behind the critical start of the school year. I walked him through the consequence of that risk and we quickly decided that he must get the project completed on time, even if it meant paying a large premium for the labor in the last week of construction. The cost of housing students in hotels, combined with the cost of lost tenants and lost income would far exceed the premium for an electrician to complete the work needed to get the building's occupancy certificate. In the end, at the start of university he was 99% complete with only a few punch list items to be completed. These could be considered warranty items and did not affect the move-in date for students. He achieved 80% occupancy by the start of school, and continued to get 3 showings and one lease signing per day to complete the project on time. This is how a time based risk can translate into massive financial risk.

A Cost risk can either be a one time impact or a recurring ongoing impact. For example, if a building renovation project encounters a problem with insulation, you might suffer a one-time impact of adding insulation to the building. Conversely, if you don't upgrade the insulation, you will face a lifetime of higher heating and air conditioning costs.

Another example might be when a property is built too close to a property line. Some building codes would require the windows on that side of the building to be fire rated windows that cost twice as much as regular windows. However, some building code rules might allow for a regular window provided the window is less than a specific surface area. At that point, you could face a choice between a larger more expensive window, or a smaller window that doesn't need to be fire rated.

The final risk category is that of quality. This is often the area that suffers when risk management is ignored, or when a project comes under stress. Poor quality is often the result of a rush to save time, cost, or both. The loss of quality can sometimes be the result of substitution of materials, or cutting corners in the process of manufacturing. For example, I live in a lovely home that was the model home for a well-respected builder. At the back of our home is a deck that extends from our kitchen and our dining room across that back of our home. The deck is supported by columns on one side and is supported by a beam that is attached to the house on the other. However, the builder did not properly install the support beam. They merely nailed it into the side of the house with a total of 19 nails over the span of 22 feet. These nails were not into the structural beams that form part of the structure of the house. Instead they were nailed into the exterior sheathing of the house which is not designed to carry the load of a deck. Slowly over the years the deck has been sinking close to the house. Quality risks often translate into cost risks or become the subject of lawsuits down the road. This is when there is a gap between expectation and reality.

How do you manage risk properly? It's a 5 step process.

1) Enumerate the potential risks
2) Qualify the risks (Time, feasibility, cost, quality)
3) Determine the likelihood
4) Quantify the impact if the risk comes true
5) Develop contingency plans for the risks with the highest impacts.

Whenever you have something that puts the project at significant risk, you have a duty to embed the contingency plan into your main-stream plan of record. That is, you have a duty to eliminate it as a risk by making it part of the plan.

Exit Strategy

An investment with no exit strategy is a prison sentence for your money. Most savvy investors want to know how they will get their money out. A realistic exit strategy is critical to enticing an investor to putting their money to work. There are several common exit strategies.

1) Business or asset sale
2) Sale of shares
3) Refinance

With an outright sale of the business or an asset, the buyer is a party unrelated to the original project. They will demand a full due diligence, and will often be looking for a "deal" relative to comparable opportunities in the market. The buyer will likely be a financial buyer or a strategic buyer. A financial buyer is essentially concerned with the numbers. A strategic buyer will be concerned with the underlying business, but may also be interested because it adds strategic value to a complementary business. An example of a strategic purchase might be a restaurant that buys retail commercial space instead of renting. They're interested in buying a piece of real estate at a good price, but the other considerations become paramount such as location, parking, who are the neighboring businesses, foot traffic, and so on. They don't need to buy the property at a discount to the market for it to make sense financially.

In some cases, the sale of the business isn't an outright sale. It consists of a sale of a portion of the outstanding shares to a partner or a new investor. The sale of shares internally will generally be a simple process and won't require extensive due diligence since the other shareholders have been involved in the project for some time.

A refinance isn't a true exit. It's more of an interim exit that enables the project to be recapitalized through the injection of new debt. That debt can be used to pay down other loan obligations or repayment of equity to shareholders.

No discussion of exit strategy would be complete without discussing structure.

There is a fourth exit strategy that is not as common, but equally powerful. If you can treat the equity investment simultaneously as a loan and an equity investment you can borrow some of the features of both types of instruments. Some types of loans have their principals repaid over a period of time using the residual cash flow of the business as the means to repay the loan. The equity component gives the equity investor a share of ownership of the business with all the rights and benefits that come with ownership. But there are many different types of shares.

- Common Shares
- Non-voting Shares
- Preferred Shares
- Convertible Shares
- Retractable Shares
- Par Value Shares
- Restricted Shares

Each of these share classes have different rights. You can bet that the distribution of profits will vary widely from one share class to the other. We devote an entire chapter to the subject of deal structure. This is so important that it makes the difference between making or losing money, irrespective of how successful the venture is.

What is the tax consequence?

The tax code in Canada and the US is massive and complex,

consisting of thousands of pages of legislation. We can't do a deep dive into tax consequence in this book. Moreover, I'm not an accountant. So please don't take accounting or tax advice from me. I'm not qualified. I will give an illustrative examples of tax decisions that could affect the willingness of an investor to put their cash into an enterprise.

Section 1031 Capital Gains Shelter

Sometimes the investor is looking to use monies that are part of an IRS code Section 1031 exchange. This is a tax sheltering of a previous investment from capital gains. Canada does not have a similar mechanism. Under the rules of section 1031, the seller must identify the potential replacement asset with 45 days of the sale of the property, and must close on the new purchase within 180 days of the prior sale. There are a number of restrictions on a 1031 exchange.

The replacement property must be of "like kind". That is to say, an investment property can be replaced with another investment property. The ownership title of the replacement property must be identical to the ownership title for the relinquished property. The replacement property must be of equal or greater value to the relinquished property.

Let's imagine that your funding partner just sold a property and they're sitting on $1,000,000 in cash. They don't want to pay the capital gains tax on their sale, so they're looking for somewhere to put their money to work and shelter it from tax. If they plan to shelter the funds using a 1031 exchange, then they will need to be on title for their share of the funding. That may give your funding partner an effective "veto" on any transactions by virtue of being on title, even if they only own 10% of the subject property. Their signature will be required on most items involving recording of deeds, mortgages, and the like.

If there isn't a match between the goals of the investor under section 1031 and the entrepreneur looking to raise capital, it simply won't work. The investor will either lose their tax exemption or they will force the entrepreneur to perform un-natural and perhaps unacceptable transactions in order to preserve the tax exempt status for the investor.

Some assets generate different types of income. The income tax act assigns a different marginal tax rate depending on the class of income. These tax rates also vary depending on where you live.

For example, in Canada passive income such as simple interest is taxed at the highest marginal tax rate. In the US, the same interest income is taxed at a much lower marginal tax rate. In Canada, active business income is taxed at the lowest marginal tax rate whereas in the US, the opposite is true. The taxation treatment will make some investments either more or less attractive depending on the amount of tax liability associated with the investment. This becomes part of the total equation in assessing whether an investment is suitable for the particular investor.

9 The Art of the Pitch

When people buy a product, or a project, or an opportunity, they're really buy you. Unless the entrepreneur has the confidence, passion, and quiet calm to ably answer any question, it will be difficult to instill that same level of confidence in the investor.

Lakshmi Balachandra conducted a painstaking analysis of the video of 185 venture capital pitches. She looked at both verbal and non-verbal factors. The results were surprising. The strongest predictor of whether the venture got funded was not the person's credentials or the content of the pitch. The strongest predictors of who got the money were concentrated in three traits: confidence, comfort level, and passionate enthusiasm. Those who succeeded did not spend their precious time worrying about what others thought of them, or how they were doing. They were fully engaged and present in the conversation.

This result isn't that surprising actually. There are many situations when we are subjected to a power imbalance. When we are asking permission, asking the bank for a loan, asking for a doctor for a medical diagnosis, appealing a tax ruling, these are all cases where the other side is in the power position. It may seem strange to protect your power position when it appears that you have none in that situation. I'm not talking about unbridled arrogance. That's never attractive or welcome in any situation. There's a quiet confidence that comes from a deeper sense of self that is not dependent on approval of others.

The pitch has a simple structure that must address 7 elements. These 7 elements are universal for most ventures. I've used this structure to pitch to venture capitalists, private equity firms, and corporate boards.

1) The Wider Market Opportunity and the Specific Short Term Opportunity
2) The Core Team and Why it's the Right Team
3) The Competitive Landscape – (Why will we win?)
4) Customer Engagement (Proof of #1)
5) The Financial Projection
6) Financial Sources and Uses
7) The Risks and Mitigation

Traditional business schools talk about the need for a business plan document. In my experience, no money manager I've worked with has ever read a business plan document in the past 15 years. I've managed to raise significant sums for new ventures and buyouts without the traditional business plan. However, a PowerPoint presentation that addresses the 7 elements I've named above has been instrumental. I've used this structure in Silicon Valley with Venture Capitalists. I've coached clients with this approach to secure funding for their company expansions.

I've seen so many pitches from startups that start with a huge market opportunity. They sound something like this....

> *"The opportunity is $1B. Our plan is to start by getting 1% of the market, so we're going to start with a $10M revenue stream. After all, it's only 1%. How hard can it be to get 1%? That's a conservative business assumption."*

Well, it turns out that getting 1% of a market is incredibly hard. If you're good enough to get 1%, then really should be able to get 25%. Furthermore, when addressing any market opportunity, large or small, you have to be laser focused on the specific need of your target clients. If you're too general, customers are unlikely to engage.

The second common mistake that I see entrepreneurs make is to try and bootstrap their business to growth. That is to say,

> *"We will start out with one employee, then two, then grow to three. We only need the seed capital to grow to the next stage. The growth of the business will take care of things from there."*

The problem with this approach is that the business is operating below critical mass in terms of skills. Businesses require complementary skills. Without the revenue to afford the skills in sales, marketing, customer service, operations, quality assurance, finance, the business will struggle to grow beyond the small confines of the self-employed. I'm not saying it's impossible, just extremely rare and difficult. Moreover, it leaves the investor feeling that you're not ready to be successful. You're thinking too small. If faced with explosive growth, your mindset will be stuck in small and will prevent the business from achieving its potential.

The 7 Elements of the Pitch are so critical that you can't raise money without it. That doesn't mean that you're going to present the pitch in linear fashion with a stuffy PowerPoint presentation. But you had better prepare and know the answers to these critical questions so that you can answer them at any time in any order, frontwards, backwards or upside down. You don't get multiple chances to make a good first impression.

The Impromptu Cell Phone Pitch

In early February of 2004, I had received an introduction to a senior executive at IBM. He was responsible for a $17 billion segment of the company at the time. We believed that a small microprocessor business of about $50 million in revenue within that $17 billion segment should be divested and we were just the company to take it off their hands.

It was about 4PM and I was walking down the sidewalk in downtown Ottawa on a snowy, busy, noisy street. My cell phone rang, and Mike Denick who headed the mergers and acquisitions for the Server and Technology Group at IBM was on the phone. He introduced himself, and said "I'm told that I'm supposed to call you".

There were trucks driving past me, taxis were honking their horns. I'm thinking to myself. "Wow, this is my one and only opportunity and I'm on a noisy sidewalk."

So I ducked into the lobby of the Royal Bank where there were about eight ATM banking machines. There was the beep of the banking machines in the background, but at least it was a little quieter.

Here's what I said:

> "Mike, I'm the Chief Operating Officer of Somerset Technologies. It's clear that IBM has achieved great success in the game console arena with Nintendo, Sony Playstation IV, and the Xbox 360. You've obviously had to move key resources internally onto those projects and it's absolutely the right thing to do for IBM. The embedded microprocessor business (where the talent came from) is suffering as a result. The embedded processor business a good business for IBM, but not a great business. I'd like to discuss partnership opportunities that could range from helping IBM support the existing customers, to the outright acquisition of the business."

His response to me was, "What if I told you it's not for sale?"

> I shot back with, "You have some tier 1 customers including Hewlett Packard, Siemens, Nokia, Cisco, Broccade, Panasonic that are going to become dissatisfied with IBM because you're ignoring these products. Again, it's absolutely the right thing for IBM to do. You have no choice. This business can't be of strategic value to IBM. It's too small. But it's large enough to be of strategic interest and central focus to us. That's why you need a partner."

He finally relented and said, "We would consider selling it. There are in fact seven other companies looking at it right now. You're late to the party. If you can send me a written Expression of Interest document which outlines what you're proposing, we'll review it and consider you as a potential. But I have to warn you that you're very late and there are much larger companies ahead of you in line."

The proposal document we sent followed the 7 step formula that I outlined above. When Mike Denick called me the next time, he was flabbergasted. He said, "Your proposal addressed 95% of what we are looking for in a partner. You must have had inside information. There's no other way you could made a proposal that was so close to what we were looking for."

We took a risk. We talked with a lot of people prior to preparing our takeover plan. Many of the people we hired had worked for direct competitors of IBM in the same space. So while we didn't know the products intimately, we knew the customers and their needs. We were ultimately invited into exclusive negotiation with IBM as a result of that process. The IBM team are among the most sophisticated business managers we're ever encountered.

In parallel with convincing IBM to sell us the business, we had to convince a private equity group to fund the purchase. We didn't have $200 million in our back pocket. Here are the 7 steps to the pitch in more detail.

In order to convince a funding partner to invest, you need to demonstrate a good understanding of your market.

The Market Opportunity

This is where you talk about the key customers and the very specific problems that you're solved for them. You show that you understand the customer's pain and how valuable the solution to their pain will be. You talk about the value of the globally available market, and the segment of the addressable market in the short term.

The Core Team and Why its the Right Team

I've sat in the board room and listened to many pitches from startup companies. Invariably after the pitch is over and we're debriefing on what we saw, someone would say "Great idea. Wrong team. If we engage with them, who would we get to lead it?" I can't emphasize this enough. If you don't have the right people in the right chairs, you won't get the money. This comes down to raising capital element #3, "Results". It's the track record of the people in each of the key roles that counts, in addition to the track record of the company. If the venture is a new business idea, then the corporate track record doesn't apply and you have to fall back on the track record of the individuals.

The Competitive Landscape – (Why will we win?)

This is critical. If there is a dominant player with strong customer relationships, you will need to be 10x better than the incumbent to push them out. Customers won't break a relationship with an existing supplier for a 10% improvement, or even a 30% improvement. It's not enough. If the competitor is much larger than you, they can exert market leverage in ways that you can't imagine. I'm reminded of Richard Branson's attempt to break into the Cola market with Virgin Cola in 1994. Coca Cola was a much larger player with very deep pockets. They could afford to wage a price war, or some other competitive tactic to try and kill Virgin. Coke's legal counsel convinced the company to be very careful with wielding its muscle in the marketplace. They risked an anti-trust investigation from the Justice Department.

Instead, Coca Cola told all their customers, that if they chose to sell Virgin Cola, they would withdraw all the Coke family products from the shelves and allow them to sell only Virgin products. This was very generous of Coke to back away and allow Virgin to walk in and take the market. The retailers realized quickly that Virgin didn't have the breadth of product line, the distribution channel, nor the brand strength to replace the revenues they would lose from Coke. In the end, Virgin admitted defeat and Coke maintained its dominant market position.

The competitive landscape is critical in understanding how you will win. This is a game of chess. Show your funding partner that you've planned three moves ahead.

Customer Engagement (Proof of #1)

Theory is nice. You've demonstrated that you understand the market dynamics and the problem you're trying to solve. Now you need to show social proof. This is where credible independent customers say how much they love your solution, and how much better it is than the competition. If you don't have this, getting funding will be very difficult.

Have you ever noticed that many products sold online have large sections of their website devoted to customer reviews? This is the same mechanism at play. It's more powerful to have a customer say how great you are, rather than bragging how great you are.

There are two types of early adopter customers that you can talk about at this stage. The first are the true early adopters who have taken your product and started using it. The second type are the advisory customers who aren't ready to adopt your product, but they are representative of the target customers and they're willing to invest the time to provide the feedback and guidance the product development process needs to make sure the product is ideal when it hits the market.

The Financial Projection

This is the classical Pro-Forma financial projection that is taught in all the business schools. The key here is to make sure the projection is grounded in reality. It's easy to get Excel to create very pretty charts and graphs. They underlying assumptions behind the projection are the part you will need to defend. You also need to include sensitivity analysis to show what happens under a couple of realistic scenarios.

Financial Sources and Uses

When you take investor monies you have a fiduciary responsibility to take good care of the money. This is when you show where the money is going to come from (Sources), and what you're going to spend it on (Uses). The sources and uses table is so standard in virtually every area of finance that it is often treated as a legal exhibit that will be used to hold management accountable.

This example shows the sources and uses table for a new construction apartment building. The metrics per square foot are also included so that the lender can calibrate the cost per square foot against industry comparable data. The lender needs to meet certain ratios to make the loan, and the sources and uses table simplifies their calculations.

SOURCES			USES		
					Cost / SF
Funding Partner(s)	$389,000	20%	Land	$225,000	$17.05
Bank Debt	$1,586,000	80%	Construction Hard Costs	$1,435,000	$108.71
			Soft Costs	$315,000	$23.86
Total Sources	$1,975,000	100%	**Total Uses**	$1,975,000	$149.62

The Risks and Mitigation

We've talked at length about risk management in chapter 7. This is where you summarize the most important risks and speak to how you'll handle them if they come true. This doesn't need to be a presentation of the full risk management plan. That's too much detail at this stage. You can offer that for the due diligence phase. When you're pitching the venture, keep the risk part of the presentation down to the top 5-6 risks and show that you're thinking about the future and how it might unfold.

The Lion King

In any negotiation there is going to be a dominant player. This is the alpha. In jungle folklore this is the lion king. Successful negotiation depends on maintaining negotiating leverage. This is a combination of real leverage, and perceived leverage. Sometimes a power imbalance exists simply because of virtual size.

In my negotiation with IBM, they were the alpha. We could easily get stepped on. They did many things to maintain their psychological leverage. We would ask the IBM team some technical questions about their products. We were conducting due diligence. We were asserting the alpha role of the buyer. At times, they would answer with "Because we're IBM". Understand that the electrons flowing through the microprocessor don't care that they were designed by IBM. That's not enough of a reason. The product will have limitations regardless who designed it. This was simply IBM trying to grab back their position of dominance.

Some people use their title to maintain the alpha role and maintain their negotiation leverage. So my question to you is:

If you were facing the President of the United States, who is the

Alpha?

You might be tempted to say that the President is in the alpha position all the time. They hold, after all, the most powerful position in the world today. But what if you were the golf coach to the President, or the President's physician? Who is the alpha in those situations? The golf coach and the doctor are clearly in the alpha role for a period of time.

There's a very important clue in examining that situation. It means that even if you're not in the most powerful position, you can still occupy the alpha role, or at least that of an equal. But in order to occupy that role, you have to bring the confidence to own it.

There are many social barriers erected to push people into the beta role and protect the position of the alpha. You will recognize them right away.

- The Power Play
- The Time Squeeze
- The Analysis Junky

These are classic methods that alphas use to exert their power. It is possible to get it back. This is usually done with a surprise disruption. It can't be mean-spirited or it will backfire. To grab power back you need to use a combination of defiance and humor. It must be done with a smile, or it will appear defensive and childish.

The Power Play is the domain of the huge ego. If you're not sure who is in the alpha position, it's easy to determine. If you are reacting to them, then they have the alpha position. If they are reacting to you, then you hold the alpha position.

The classic Time Squeeze goes something like this. "I only have 20 minutes to spend with you. Let's make it quick"

You can reply with a smile and say, "That's OK, I only have 15 minutes." This kind of disruption will break the pattern and level the playing field. The alpha will know that they are dealing with a professional who understands power dynamics.

When you are looking to raise capital, the pitch can easily and quickly devolve into analysis paralysis. When this happens, you've lost control of the pitch. If you dive deep into the numbers, you need to get control back and quickly. Here's what I would say in a situation like that:

> "Look, the revenues are $2.1 million, the expenses are $700,000, and the debt service on the property is $800,000. The net cash flow is $600,000. These are financial details that you can verify in due diligence along with many other details. In the meantime, the purpose of this meeting is to determine if we have a fit. That's what we need to work on. "

By appealing to the higher purpose, I am able to disrupt the Analysis Junky and regain control of the meeting.

The Shark Tank Effect

The TV shows like Shark Tank and Dragons Den have done a great job of educating the population at large how to pitch for money. They are reality TV shows and the teams that make it on TV are selected for a variety of reasons. First of all, it's a TV show, so it has to be entertaining. Even a train wreck can be entertaining. A great venture that doesn't make for good TV won't make it onto the show.

I auditioned for the Dragons Den TV show in 2014. I was working on a product called "Car Footprints". The idea behind the product was to have an automated way to track auto mileage for business and personal use. Every time you get in the car, an application running on your smart phone would awaken and ask you whether it are taking a business trip or personal trip. The phone would link to a Bluetooth device attached to the car's diagnostic port and provide odometer readings at regular intervals. The data from the application would integrate seamlessly with accounting software such as Quicken, Quickbooks, Excel, and Xero. I was selected to go on the show. I went to the taping and spent the majority of the day in the studio along with a dozen other entrepreneurs. My pitch went well, or so I thought. But the Dragons were looking to fund projects that had already achieved revenue. We were still in the testing phase of the product and had not released it for sale yet. As a result we didn't get funded. Sadly, my segment probably was too boring and ended up on the cutting room floor. It never aired.

Was this a failure? Yes, and No. I failed to get the money. I learned something, so that was a success. I got to experience a behind the scenes view of the show, something that very few people get to do. All of that was a monumental success. Best of all, I could pitch the project to another investor the very next day. I still had the ability to stay in the game. The only true failure is when you have to shut down a venture.

In the end, the Dragons were right about not investing in an early stage company. We found the testing matrix of car models, phone types, and software releases to be far too costly for the level of revenue that the product would generate. Each new software release on each phone platform would trigger additional development spending to keep the application working across all platforms and cars, with no new revenue to justify the additional R&D expenditure. We had made a fundamental error in understanding the lifecycle cost of developing, releasing and maintaining a product in the marketplace across a wide range of cars and devices. In the end my partner and I did not recover our investment in the product. That was a true failure. But nobody went bankrupt. The investment in the product was of a manageable size and everyone was prepared for the possibility it might not work.

There are several reasons to go on a show such as Dragons' Den or Shark Tank. Probably top of the list is market visibility. An appearance on Shark Tank pays huge dividends in terms of visibility. You don't need to get funded by the Sharks to get the benefit of being on the show.

My good friends Jarrett and Raja live in Las Vegas. They have a high energy magic and music show. Jarrett is the magician, and Raja is a concert pianist who studied piano in Ottawa Canada, and subsequently at Juilliard School in New York City. They were looking for the funds to bank-roll a high profile show on the Las Vegas strip. They were among the 143,000 applications to the show. They auditioned and were selected to have their pitch recorded during the regular season taping.

At the very moment one should be celebrating making it onto SHARK TANK to present a pitch to the investor sharks, disaster strikes, and a golden opportunity becomes a nightmare. Who thinks of setting an assistant on fire to make her vanish, then reappear as a mermaid inside an aquarium of fish built into a $10 million piano?

Jarrett & Raja have stunned audiences around the world and in TV appearances, but stardom on the Strip has eluded them. They set out to impress the Sharks and have them finance their magic production. "We want to be the next Siegfried & Roy," the guys told the sharks in looking for $750,000 in exchange for 40 percent of the show.

Raja and Jarrett knew that the Sharks had never funded anything like this before. They knew that their likelihood of getting a deal on the show was small. They did it anyway for several reasons.

1) The exposure to a wider audience
2) Practice pitching the business side of the show to investors.

There were tense moments. The aquarium broke seconds before they started recording, and water poured onto the keyboard. This happened literally 4 minutes before the start of recording. They had no idea if any sound would come out of the piano. It could have been a disaster.

However, Jarret & Raja still pulled off the trick, risking electrocution. The sharks were impressed but didn't want to finance a Las Vegas show. They were selected for Shark Tank because a large scale magic trick makes for entertaining television.

Jarrett and Raja had previously appeared on America's Got Talent. On a talent show, you're simply entertaining the audience. It's not the same as an investor pitch. On Shark Tank, the curtain was pulled back on the financial merits of the venture. They gave a truly compelling pitch. The pitch failed because it wasn't a good fit to the investing criteria of the Sharks. They were fishing in the wrong pond (forgive the pun). None of the Sharks knew anything about the finances of running a show in Vegas.

In the end, the gamble paid off. Other producers watching SHARK TANK were so amazed that they decided to contact the duo, and now the they have their own headline show called ONE EPIC NIGHT, which premiered in September 2016 at the Plaza Hotel and Casino on the Las Vegas Strip, and then moved to a new permanent show in a larger venue at Hooters Casino. The aquarium and piano have been repaired, and theatergoers and magic fans will see the trick as intended.

So why did the other producers buy it? In the words of Raja:

"After Shark Tank we were inundated with phone calls from many companies trying to "help us" by offering various marketing services. In the middle of these calls was a call from a producer who wanted us to be part of a new Vegas show. He called three times before finally connecting with us. The producer fell in love with us. He saw the potential to attract a different audience. Magic is hot these days. Just look at America's Got Talent. You have 4 magic acts in the semi-finals. That's unheard of."

The concept was originally for a music show. When he saw Jarrett and Raja's combination of magic and music together, he saw a unique differentiator that audiences would love. A new concept was created by combining Jarrett and Raja's show with two stars from "The Voice" TV show.

In the end, Jarrett and Raja got the gig and they now earn a share of the show revenues. They're more than just performers. They have the media contacts and the relationships to generate publicity for the show. The business model for a Vegas show typically achieves break-even at 30% of the potential seat sales in a 400 seat venue. Ticket sales have been steadily increasing with each and every passing week. The reviews were glowing, and they didn't get a single negative review. This is virtually unheard of in the world of entertainment. They played to their first sold out house less than two weeks after opening.

10 Is Philanthropy the Same as Business?

The biggest difference between a business and a philanthropic endeavor is the measurement of success. For a business, the measures of revenue, profitability and growth are standard fare. For a charity, the measures are much more domain specific. A charity that saves lives will be measured by the number of lives saved. A charity that restores vision to people who are blind will measure the number of people whose vision has been restored. A charity that helps people with addictions will measure the number of people who are no longer addicts.

There are several different ways to engage a charity. America's sixty-eight thousand foundations are replete with paradoxes. Foundations must be free and autonomous in order to fulfill their mission of challenging, reforming, and renewing society. At the same time, in part because of the tax benefits they enjoy, they must somehow be accountable to society. There are three possible ways charitable foundations contribute to the civic sector.

1) As a driver
2) A Catalyst
3) As a Partner

When taking a driver role, your foundation is directly attempting to solve a particular problem. That can be a huge undertaking. In some cases, government involvement is required to change policy. Let's say that you want to change an aspect human rights policy. A charitable foundation doesn't have the tools necessary to change human rights directly. In that case, the role of catalyst is to change government policy. The foundation must work through influence.

In some cases, foundations simply want to raise money towards a cause, but not do the heavy lifting of solving the problem directly. They would prefer to partner with an existing organization and support the work of the driver in a partnership. By maintaining a separate partner foundation, the donor can maintain some element of control and direct funds to one or more foundations that are working in the same area.

For example, one of my personal desires is to help people who are blind. It turns out that a large percentage of blindness can be reversed for less than $100 per person. My personal lifetime goal is to eliminate blindness for 100,000 people. Strictly speaking, that would take about $10 million. That's a drop in the bucket considering the impact. There is a very good global organization based in the UK with branch offices in the US called SightSavers. They do excellent work. If I was to raise $10 million and the go hire doctors, fly them to India and Africa, manage the logistics, and so on, my impact would be small. I can accomplish more by partnering with SightSavers and directing my giving towards an existing organization.

There are many worldwide initiatives that have been the result of philanthropy. In the 1940's Mexico had a massive food shortage. The Rockefeller Foundation started an initiative called the Green Revolution in 1945. They hired scientists to work in Mexico and create new varieties of corn, wheat and rice that were better suited to the climate. This work was so successful that Mexico was self sufficient in growing wheat by 1956, where previously they imported half of their wheat from the United States and Canada.

The first 911 emergency telephone system was set up in Alabama in 1968. It's a little known fact that the 911 emergency response system is the result of a philanthropic effort. Today, an average day in New York City sees about 35,000 E911 each and every day. Needless to say, the 911 system has had a profound impact on saving lives.

When the national 911 emergency-response system was created, the Robert Wood Johnson Foundation took the Driver role. It catalyzed and financed 911 organizations across the United States, brought together emergency responders who hadn't previously cooperated and created a uniform environment of cooperation.[1]

So why do so many charities and foundations struggle to raise money? I believe it's because the team makeup of many charitable foundations is focused on helping those in need and they don't understand the relationship between the foundation and its donors. The leadership believes that it's enough to have a worthy cause. People will line up and part with their hard earned cash because it's a worthy cause. How naive. These organizations often

---

[1] Fleishman, Joel L. (2007-01-09). The Foundation: A Great American Secret; How Private Wealth is Changing the World (p. 5).

suffer from a lack of transparency and accountability. I was speaking recently with a donor and board member at a women's shelter. She told me a story of how the executive director who lived in another city, wanted to travel to the shelter for a week to "manage the staff". The board (fortunately) denied the travel request. It would have been a $4,000 expense that would have done nothing to help those in need, and would have amounted to a $4,000 paid vacation for the executive director. Behaviors such as this can poison the fund-raising capability of a foundation for years to come.

The most successful organizations know it's far more important to demonstrate transparency and accountability in their operations. One of the best examples I'm aware of is the Eric Trump Foundation, which is partnered with St. Jude Children's Cancer Research Hospital in Memphis. The entire facility operates on a donation basis. All of the children who have the misfortune of contracting cancer are treated free of charge. Not only that, the hospital is one of the leading research facilities in the world. They ensure that all their research is NOT patented and is put into the public domain for the betterment of humanity. This was the vision of Danny Thomas, the founder of St. Jude in 1962. I'm using this example because there are two charitable organizations working in partnership. St. Jude is in the driver role. The Eric Trump foundation operates in a partner role. It was founded and managed by Eric Trump and Andrew Graves. They are a zero overhead foundation and 99.3% of the funds raised are donated to St. Jude. There is only one admin assistant drawing a salary who oversees the collection and dissemination of the funds, and organizing events. This transparency makes it easy for people to donate. They know that their funds are being put to work. Eric announced a $28 million pledge to build an expansion of the hospital in 2013. This pledge was completed well ahead of schedule. I've personally participated in several charity events with Eric. In one such event, we raised $360,000 in 90 minutes. All of the funds were in support of St. Jude. This is an example of how a partnership can provide leverage to an organization in the driver role.

Criteria for Giving to a Charity

How is it that some charitable foundations struggle to raise a few thousand dollars at a silent auction, and others manage to raise hundreds of thousands or millions in the same amount of time? It's because the successful ones understand the principles of raising capital. They understand that you need to provide a demonstrable rate of return on the funds invested (donated). It's a donation, but it's still an investment. The donors are expecting a return on their donation. They're measuring it in very similar ways to a pure financial investment.

1) How much money is needed to solve the problem?
2) What is the minimum donation to be meaningful?
3) When will the stated results happen?
4) How much of my money will reach the intended destination?
5) How do I know the efforts of the charity are actually solving the stated problem?
6) Is the foundation a registered charity and will I get a proper tax deduction for the donation?

These questions are very similar in nature to the questions being asked by investors in a business. The key elements when dealing with a charity (same as in business) are transparency and accountability.

One of my mentors taught me a lot about how to give, from his own perspective. His philosophy (and now mine) is that every donation should have a measurable result. For example, he bought an ambulance for a neonatal critical care unit. Not only did he fund the vehicle, but also all the equipment (the expensive part) needed for the ambulance to fulfill its mission. In the first two years of operation, the ambulance saved 63 lives on Long Island. That's a tangible measurable outcome.

The United Way supports many organizations that perform great work. They are good at raising money. They work in a partnership context. They benefit a number of charities that are in the driver role. But perhaps the biggest weakness is that it is very hard to provide a measurable linkage between the donation and a tangible result. The money is spread around like salt and pepper across too many agencies for the donor to truly understand the impact of their funds.

Good Cause, Bad Foundation

Some charitable foundations have also attracted their share of criticism. The Clinton Foundation stands out as the most visible example in recent memory. Certainly the polarized partisan politics surrounding the 2016 federal election have played a large role in the amount of negative press generated. When justifiable criticism of a charitable foundation occurs, there are a few "bad" behaviors at play.

1) Arrogance
2) Inaccessibility
3) Lack of Accountability
4) Failure to communicate

Some foundation owners have acted as if the funds in the foundation is "their money". By definition, if the money is destined for a cause, the foundation owner is only a steward of the money, a caretaker of it for a short time. It is a fiduciary responsibility.

Good reputations are hard to build and easy to destroy. Look at the foundations that have bad behaviors and "Don't Do That"!

The people who need the help are being adversely affected by the bad behavior of the foundation leadership. The need is still there, it's still genuine, and it's still a worthy cause. One recent example I'm familiar with is a women's shelter that is in need of major repairs. There's no money for that. The primary source of government funding disappeared, and the center is housing 60 women and their children in a space that was designed for 30. To make matters worse, the executive director is abusing their position, inadvertently turning away potential donors because of their bad behavior. Once that happens, the trust in the foundation is lost and the people in need feel abandoned. They think that people don't care about them. The truth is that people care, but have lost trust in the foundation leadership. They have no clue what the root cause of the problem is. They just see the symptom that there is no money.

Foundation leadership carries with it the same fiduciary responsibilities that caring for someone's investment requires. It doesn't have the same legal ramifications. If you abscond with investor monies, you will have the local securities commission and police department knocking on your door. On the other hand, charitable foundations can operate with much more independence because it is a "donation" not an investment. Once money is donated, it's gone. However, if you have the true interest of the underlying cause at heart, you MUST treat donor funds with the same care as investor funds. It is, after all, an investment with a social outcome rather than a financial return.

Victor J. Menasce

11 Investors are a Fickle Bunch

Investors will often make a verbal commitment to fund a project prior to completion of the legal documents. The final documents may not be completed until closing day, hours before funds are to be wired. If you're in tune with your funding partners, there will be few surprises.

However, on the rare occasion, an investor who has committed to a project will back out at the last minute. Does this mean that investors can't be trusted to deliver? Sometimes that's true. It's not that they are not trust worthy. They may not have disclosed all of the moving parts that are needed for them have liquid cash available when they committed. For example, I had an investor back out of a deal less than a week before closing. They were depending on the "firm" sale of a property to complete. The proceeds of that sale were planned to be invested in my project. When their sale fell through, it had a cascade effect on the investor's ability to participate in my project.

This particular circumstance put me in an awkward position because I had not planned on the possibility that the investor would not close. I was faced with having to raise funds with less than a week before I needed the funds. When time is short, I could risk appearing desperate to some investors. Desperation is never attractive.

The solution to avoid this situation is to raise more money than you actually need. It's a little like over-booking on airlines.

You should be talking with multiple lenders, and multiple investors at the same time. You will ultimately choose only one principal lender to work with on a project, unless the project is so large that you will need to syndicate multiple lenders together. That means you will eventually choose one and say "Thank you, next time" to the rest. Maintaining a relationship and trust with the ones who are sitting out the project is crucial. You never know when you might need them in the future.

Dealing with equity investors is a little different. Your capital stack is likely going to be comprised of a combination of equity, mezzanine funds and debt. Most of your capital raising efforts are going to be focused on the equity side of the equation. That's the scarce commodity. Debt is more readily available once you understand the criteria that need to be met for a wide variety of lenders to engage on competitive terms.

Let's say you've designed your capital stack as 80% debt and 20% equity. Let's say for example that you decide to raise 25% equity in order to ensure that you meet your 20% goal.

In the case of airlines, on a rare occasion, someone doesn't get a seat on the plane. The key to managing a situation like this is to ensure that you don't lose trust with customers who don't get a seat. You could have the same issue with the one or two investors who might have to sit out a particular project.

One option might be to relax your financial model and accept a slightly higher equity ratio and reduce the amount of debt. The downside of this approach is that you end up reducing your own equity in the project by allowing more equity investors into the venture than you strictly require.

You've designed your capital stack in a manner that gives a percentage of equity to the entrepreneur, perhaps some equity to key employees, and equity to the investors. If you allow more investors into the project than needed, the equity to compensate the investors needs to come from somewhere. This means taking it from your own share as the entrepreneur. If you as the entrepreneur have, say, a 75% share of the venture, then it might be possible to give an extra 5% to investors and reduce your share to 70%. But if you've designed your share such that you're at 51%, giving up controlling share might be more difficult. In that case, you may have to tell one or two investors that you're fully subscribed and unfortunately they can't invest.

This may pose a dilemma. Should you grant the additional investors a share, and risk losing control? Perhaps maintaining control even at the expense of delaying a few investors opportunity to invest would be the better choice.

Regardless, it's wise to have a plan A, plan B, plan C, as many as you need to ensure the venture will be successful. If you are over-subscribed, put them first in line for the next opportunity if you can't accommodate them immediately.

12 Great Teams Row in the Same Direction

In order for any business relationship to withstand the test of time and real world problems, there must be alignment of goals. The fit between the business and the investor has to be completely natural. If there's any aspect that appears forced, it won't work. If there is a scenario that's win-lose for either side, it won't work. I'm a huge believer in win-win scenarios. There may be highly successful entrepreneurs who disagree with me on this point. I'm perfectly comfortable with that notion. Sometimes win-lose scenarios are unavoidable, but as much as possible you want to make sure they don't enter into your business practices, even if you're on the winning side.

Win-win has a very extensive meaning. It means that a number of critical test questions have been asked of the key stakeholders in the business. This extends beyond investor relations into the core business team itself. As an entrepreneur, your job is to recruit the best possible team in the world. The same alignment that you need with investors must also exist internally. If the team isn't aligned, then they won't be rowing in the same direction.

For example, let's imagine that the core team members in a business are three decades apart in age. Such a large age gap between core team members can be problematic. The younger team member is naturally going to be biased towards reinvesting for the future growth of the business. The older team member who is near retirement, or perhaps older is going to have a harvesting mindset. Cash flow will be more important than reinvesting for growth. There are other examples of critical cultural alignment points. Issues of work ethic, initiative, accountability, communication styles and compensation systems are all core, values based decisions that must be made and aligned.

Of all of these, perhaps the largest cultural norm to establish is around accountability. People love to hold others accountable, but sometimes don't like it when they themselves are held to the same standard. This double standard can spell disaster for a team. It can poison an environment and make substandard performance acceptable. We get what we tolerate in life, and in business. If we tolerate excuses, we will get excuses. If we tolerate procrastination, we will get procrastination. If we tolerate poor customer service, you guessed it. Whenever something isn't working in a business, the key is to raise the standards of performance.

In the book "The Wisdom of Teams", authors Jon Katzenbach and Doug Smith describe the four stages of team development:

1. Forming
2. Storming
3. Norming
4. Performing

It's vitally important for teams to pass through the storming phase and actually deal with the difficult questions affecting the business and team performance. Only once these tough conversations have taken place, can new business cultural norms be established. Governance rules that are universally accepted and embraced by the organization are essential. These rules must have consensus amongst the leadership team. Employees don't get a say in governance. Business isn't a democracy. Consensus by definition isn't the same as unanimity. It's a state where all the key stakeholders have had the opportunity to voice their opinions. The decision is one where all the key stakeholders can live with the outcome and agree to support the decision. A democratic vote is actually the lowest form of consensus. In a vote, there are winners and losers. The losers' voices are silenced. Consensus has the full support and buy-in of the stakeholders. It ensures that all the members of the executive team are rowing in the same direction.

Strong leadership also requires a single leader to make decisions that the entire organization aligns with. Again, a business isn't a democracy. Many companies have achieved monumental success with an autocratic benevolent dictator at the helm. Apple's monumental success was the result of Steve Jobs introducing the iPod, the Apple Stores, then the iPhone, then the iPad. Each one of these major decisions were made with the creative input of many talented people which was used to inform a series of decisions by a single leader.

Investors need to understand how decisions are made in an organization in order to develop confidence in the ongoing ability of the company to make great decisions. There needs to be a level of transparency.

The landscape is littered with companies that self destructed from the inside because they spent more energy fighting internal battles than fighting the battle in the marketplace. Winning in the market is the only battle that counts.

Savvy investors know that team dynamics can be challenging. Jim Collins did an extensive study of 1,435 companies in corporate America in his book "Good to Great". In that book he was looking for the ingredients that made companies excel.

So much of North American corporate culture is based on the idea of a rock star leader. Think of Apple, Ford, Virgin, Microsoft. The research was surprising, and the results were unexpected. But the findings in the data were inescapable. In reality, the most successful companies in making massive sustained growth over a period of decades had what Jim Collins calls level 5 leaders.

Level 5 leaders channel their ego needs away from themselves and into the larger goal of building a great company. It's not that level 5 leaders have no ego or self-interest. On the contrary, they're highly ambitious. But their ambition is first and foremost for the company, and not for themselves.

Geoff Smart describes the qualities needed for a successful hire in his book called "Who. The A Method for Hiring"

There are 5 main qualities.

1) Chemistry
2) Coachable
3) Smarts to do the Job
4) Commitment
5) Ego in Check

Traditional HR tends to focus very heavily on skills. This is a huge mistake. At Starbucks they hire for personal attributes because they can teach anyone to make coffee. But if you don't like to interact with people, if you're not polite and cheerful, Starbucks can't teach you that.

Richard Branson started an airline with absolutely zero domain knowledge. If there was ever an industry on the planet that is steeped in deep domain knowledge, it's the airline industry. He made the decision to start an airline. His first phone call was to the toll free number at Boeing and he asked to speak with a salesman. His attitude was "I'm a smart guy. I'll hire smart people. We're not inventing anything new here. How hard can it be?" Too much emphasis is placed on experience rather than attributes.

Donald Trump interviewed dozens of highly credentialed hotel managers when he opened his hotel in Las Vegas. In the end, he handed the job to his chauffeur. He knew that his chauffeur had the grit and persistence to make anything work, no matter how difficult. That was the quality that he simply could not train or acquire through experience. You either have it or you don't.

There are countless examples of businesses that have hired "the perfect experience" only to be disappointed with the result. Experience is important, but is actually the fifth and last attribute. All five attributes must be there for a successful hire.

13 Organic versus Non-organic Growth

There are three ways to grow a business organically.

1) Get more customers.
2) Raise your prices.
3) Sell existing customers more stuff.

True business growth depends on number one and number three. Both of these processes take considerable time. If you want your business to grow faster than it can naturally grow through regular marketing and sales, then buying a business or product line could be the way to go. I'm a strong advocate of growth by acquisition. However, acquisitions are also fraught with pitfalls. A large percentage of acquisitions fail. In those cases, the acquiring company failed to properly integrate the people and the culture of the two organizations.

Certain types of businesses lend themselves better to acquisition than others. For example, accounting firms, law firms, property management firms, real estate brokerages are all examples of service based businesses that have little client overlap. They are extremely easy to integrate. The local teams are generally able to remain intact with little disruption from the acquisition.

Product businesses where the product of the acquired company are incorporated into the product of the parent company are more difficult, but still can be successful. The problem lies in the support of the existing customers of the acquired business. The main purpose of the acquisition was to buy a piece of technology that would complement and strengthen the product line of the parent company.

Startup companies often focus on angel investors or venture capital as a means to raise funds. Private equity firms and hedge funds are the funding source of choice for acquisitions. Companies at the top tier of private equity include The Blackstone Group, The Carlyle Group, Bain Capital, Francisco Partners, Texas Pacific Group, Golden Gate Capital, Fortress Capital to name just a few. These companies will often make acquisitions possible and will ensure that the principals have enough equity to remain interested. This means that the principals can expect anywhere from 10%-20% ownership in the resulting new venture. The private equity firm may also further leverage their investment by asking the company to take on a percentage of traditional business debt. This will have the effect of reducing profitability, because of the added interest expense. But if the leverage is sufficient, the benefit outweighs the extra expense for the investor.

Rollups

It's possible to create tremendous value through acquisition. The concept of corporate value is a function of earnings multiples.

Earnings multiples are a function of size and scale. Small companies might be valued at 1-3 times earnings. Large publicly traded companies can trade anywhere from 10-30 times earnings depending on their track record and growth trajectory. By adding scale, you can often create value by the double effect of increasing the earnings, combined with the effect of a larger earnings multiple.

There is an entire industry dedicated to performing this kind of financial engineering. Private equity firms will purchase small to medium sized businesses that integrate easily. These "roll-ups" create value by eliminating redundancy that comes from having multiple head office staff, multiple sales organizations competing for the same customers, subsequently rationalized to a single head office staff and a single sales organization. These savings can often double the profitability of a company.

The second dimension of value creation results when the marketplace recognizes that a larger company will command a higher earnings multiple. Two small companies valued each at three times earnings could be combined into a single company valued at 5 times earnings. Let's look at a specific example.

Consider two property management firms. Firm A is called Sunshine property management. It has 400 units under management at an average of annual revenue of $2,000 per unit. Annual revenue is approximately $800,000 per year. The company has property managers, accounting staff, leasing agent, full-time maintenance staff, and executive management. The company is generating net operating profit margins of 20% or approximately $160,000 a year. At its present size, the company is worth approximately 3x earnings or just about $480,000

The second firm is called Multi Rental Management. It has 1,100 units under management. It too is bringing revenue of approximately $2,000 per unit per year. Total annual revenue is $2.2M. Net earnings are about 25% of revenue or $550,000. It's worth about 4x net earnings of $550,000 or $2.2M. Basically it can be bought for 1 year's revenue.

By purchasing both companies, it's possible to save approximately $200,000 a year in operating expense after combining the two companies together. This will increase the combined earnings of the two companies to $910,000 and total combined revenue remains unchanged at $3M.

But watch what happens. At $3M or more, the value of the company increases to 5x earnings. Now the combined company is worth $4.5M, but previously was only worth just under $2.7M. There was nearly $1.9M of value created by simply merging the two revenue streams together.

There is a trend in property management firms of consolidation in the industry. Once a firm reaches 2000 units under management, it's ready to be acquired by a hedge fund looking to do a larger scale roll-up. Hedge funds are offering 6x earnings as a price multiple. They know that once they aggregate about $20 million a year in revenue, they can further improve the efficiency, increase the profit margin above 30%, and get a 10x multiple through a public offering.

Not all companies lend themselves well to growth by acquisition. But many service businesses do. Laidlaw was a company under CEO Mike DeGroote that grew dramatically in the 1980's under his watch through acquisition. The company was primarily in waste disposal and school bussing. By buying waste disposal (garbage trucking) firms and school bus fleets, they could grow with little cultural conflict. A school bus driver in Ohio will have little interaction with a school bus driver in Manitoba. These parts of the business operate largely independently of one another. The revenue stream was highly predictable and based on long term contracts with school boards and municipal waste management departments. Once they had a long term contract, the company would have to perform badly in order to lose it. Growth through increasing fees was very limited. Growth by trying to get more repeat business was impossible since it was governed by long term contracts. Getting more clients through traditional sales tactics was also difficult since cities and school boards rarely switched suppliers. Growth by buying competitors was really the only way. As long as the acquisition strategy delivered sufficient improvements in efficiency, and the company had the ability to raise capital, the strategy was easy. That's the power of raising capital to grow your business.

Product Line Extensions

Let's say that you're in the business of manufacturing pepper grinders for commercial restaurant applications. You offer these products with the restaurant's name and logo laser etched onto the product. You decide to expand into selling salt shakers and salt grinders. That would be a natural product line extension. The incremental development cost to add salt to the product line is small. This should be done internally and grow the business organically.

But let's say that you want to now add table top candles, oil lamps, novelty drink glasses, balsamic vinegar dispensers, all branded with the restaurant logo. There is significantly more development required to bring those products to market. You might find another company offering those products in a different geography. By buying the second company you would have the dual benefit of expanding the product line, together with expanding the geographic reach of the company. Let's look at some numbers to see how this would work.

Business #1: Pepper Grinders International

Revenue:	$3,000,000
Manpower:	15
Expenses:	$2,200,000
Profit:	$800,000
Geographic reach:	USA, from East coast to Colorado
Profit Margin:	26%

Business #2: Restaurant Glassware

Revenue:	$5,000,000
Manpower:	30
Expenses:	$4,000,000
Profit:	$1,000,000
Geographic reach:	USA, West of Mississippi
Profit Margin:	20%

By combining the two companies, they were able to add the revenues for a total of $8M. In addition, there was a portion of the sales organization that overlapped in the middle of the country. This was rationalized for a saving of $80,000. The head office staff also had some redundancy for a further saving of $150,000. Combined expenses were $5,900,000. This improved the blended margin to 26.25% overall.

But the real benefit came from leveraging the existing sales channels across the country to sell more product through the same channel to the same customers. After two years of expanded product offering, the combined revenue grew to $12,000,000, with no increase in staff. The expenses grew as a result of more inventory flowing through the combined company for a total of $8,300,000. Profit margin increased to 30.5%.

Combined Business after two years:

Revenue: $12,000,000

Manpower: 42

Expenses: $8,300,000

Profit: $3,700,000

Geographic reach: USA country wide

Profit Margin: 30.5%

Combined profit increased from $1,800,000 to $3,700,000. The revenue increased by 50%, but the profit increased by 100%. Since valuation of a company is based on multiples of net income, the value of the company also increased by 100% in two years.

This kind of growth would have been virtually impossible to achieve through natural organic growth alone. That's the power of growth through acquisition.

Industry Transformations

Many startups are based on an idea that could transform an industry. The problem with these businesses is that they offer a great idea, but lack the revenue, momentum, and scale to survive the perilous ascent from startup to credible competitor in the market.

I prefer to consider buying a customer, or a potential partner company that is in the same industry. Let's look at a simple example. Let's imagine you just invented the zipper. You want to form a startup company to develop and market all kinds of zippers. Large steel zippers for luggage, skinny nylon zippers for women's dresses, short ones for pants, and long ones for ski bags and tents.

My recommendation would be to buy a company that sells buttons. They already have a channel to market established. Many of the button customers would also buy zippers. The revenue stream from buttons would provide the cash needed to develop all the zipper variants that the market demands.

In this scenario, you are buying the button business based on the value of its existing business. The potential value of the business to multiply its revenue by putting more products through the same channel becomes part of your value creation. This value proposition is highly attractive to a financial buyer. If the acquisition target is marginally profitable, or perhaps slightly losing money, it might be possible to buy the business at a deep discount. The value creation from the sale of zippers will be enough to make the company wildly profitable and create huge returns for the investors. As the entrepreneur, you're creating an industry transformation. For the investor, it's called a business turnaround. These scenarios as relatively easy to get funded because they're so compelling. The business is a going concern. It has revenue, customers, track record. The degree of speculation is nicely contained to whether the product line extension will be successful. This is a much lower risk scenario than a startup that has no revenue and no customers.

How do you prepare to buy a business? You need to know a lot of inside information about the acquisition target to know whether it will be a fit or not.

My personal corporate buy-out experience

How do you identify these opportunities? Sometimes the business isn't a standalone business. Major corporations often spin off assets that are not core to their strategy. For example, I was directly involved in the purchase of three different product lines from IBM and Motorola. In one case, the product from IBM represented about $12M a year in revenue annually. For a company the size of IBM, $12M was a rounding error, a distraction. The business had the potential to grow to about $30-$40M per year. Even if it achieved its objective, it would still be a rounding error and a distraction. So it made sense for IBM to divest of the asset. I learned a lot from that process. There are numerous stakeholders in an acquisition.

1) The investors
2) The employees at the parent company
3) The employees at the company being acquired
4) The customers of both companies

The transition plan needs to explicitly address the needs of all the stakeholders. This includes a communication plan, and a plan for regular follow-up with each group over the first 6-12 months following the acquisition.

As a result of that experience, I put together another startup company designed to acquire another product line from IBM. In this case, it was a larger acquisition consisting of their embedded microprocessor division. This group had about 100 customers worldwide and was achieving about $50M a year in revenue. In order to convince IBM to sell to us, and to convince our financial backers, we needed to convince both of them that we had the right team with the right expertise. This consisted of showing that all of the key people had played similar roles in similar businesses and sold to the same customers.

The second step was to show that we had a well-considered business transition plan. An acquisition is different than a startup. It's an instant business and you need to have the right people in the right chairs performing at 100% right away. You don't have the luxury of six months of on-the-job training for the rookies. So we had to hire slightly over-qualified people to occupy all of the key leadership roles in the organization. By doing so, we instilled confidence that we had a winning team. At the end of the day, having the right team is the only way that the investors would see a return on their investment. They could perform due diligence on the asset to make sure it was being purchased at an attractive price.

The third step was to show IBM that we had carefully considered the need to protect the IBM brand. If we stumbled with the customers, they would get mad at IBM more than us.

After we took over the IBM business, we went on a tour and physically visited each of the key customers. Those smaller customers we could not economically visit, we scheduled phone calls to introduce ourselves and establish personal points of contact. We assigned ownership of key customers to each member of the senior management team. That executive member was tasked with the role of customer advocate for each of the key customers. This made it possible to spread the burden of customer retention across the senior management team. Sales and support people were also assigned to each customer. Having an executive escalation path was critical to showing each customer that they were valued and that they weren't being dumped by IBM. This was part of what we needed to do to keep the customers engaged, and it had the side effect of protecting the IBM brand at the same time. That was one of the criteria of the acquisition.

14 Deal Structure

I'll give you any price you want as long as I get to dictate the terms. Don't believe me? Yes, I'll agree pay you $1,000,000,000 for that 1993 vintage rusty car with 300,000 miles on the odometer.

> "I'll pay you $0.01 per day until the car is paid in full."

Deal structure is all about the terms under which a deal gets done. It defines who gets paid first, when they get paid, and under what conditions. Who ultimately profits from a venture is defined almost exclusively by the deal structure.

> Can you lose money from a profitable venture? Yes.

> Can you profit from a money losing venture? Yes.

Deal structure is the most important part of any negotiation. Ignore it at your peril. It defines who is in control and under what circumstances.

Let's look at a simple example. Let's say that a business is generating $1M a year in revenue, and $100,000 a year in profit. The investor wants to get $50,000 a year in income from the business. This could be expressed as:

1. 5% of the gross revenue = $50,000

2. 50% of the net profit = $50,000

3. A $50,000 preferred payment

All three statements initially yield the same $50,000 payment. But they're vastly different in reality.

In case #1, the company could double in revenue to $2M per year. But it could also increase expenses such that it's ultimately losing money, and now the payment due to the investor would be $100,000.

In case #2, the revenue could drop by 10% while expenses remain fixed, wiping out any profit, and giving the investor zero.

Case #3, will give the investor $50,000 no matter what else is happening in the business.

Which one should you pick? It depends. There is no single right answer. It's a matter of negotiating a complete set of terms and conditions between the investors and the business that are fair and balanced to all parties. Each one of these examples could be considered a win-lose deal.

It's all about achieving alignment between the various divergent needs of a venture. Even when there is alignment, you have to acknowledge that there are divergent needs, a virtual tug of war over the same money.

- Company wants to charge customers more
- Customers want to pay less
- Employees want higher salaries

- Owners and investors want to reduce operating expenses

- Investors want a higher rate of return

- Some investors want the business to swap equity for third party debt, but retain ownership interest.

- Owners want to re-invest profits in expansion of the business

All of these interests are fighting over the same dollars. There are multiple stakeholders at the table involved in the discussion simultaneously. There are so many moving parts it can make your head spin. This is complicated stuff. There are so many ways for problems to creep into a set of agreements. We could never cover all the possible cases in this book. But we can instill a mind-set that enables you critically examine a situation and create a structure that is fair to all parties. Sometimes, even very smart people make some very serious well intentioned mistakes.

Oops, Honey I accidentally sold the company

I was recently speaking with the CEO of a company that was negotiating a large investment. The investor was a representative of a wealthy family and was negotiating on behalf of the family. The investment being contemplated was over $1B dollars. As such, the investor asked that the company not seek any alternate sources of financing. The CEO agreed and signed an exclusivity agreement with the investor.

When I dug into the situation with the CEO, it was clear that they had not yet reach agreement with the wealthy investor on the terms of an investment. Moreover, there was no expiry terms set on the exclusivity agreement. Basically, the investor could dictate when the company had the right to seek alternate financing.

Under these terms, the investor had 100% control of the company without having spend even $1 of investment in the company. They held all the negotiating leverage, and the company had no right to seek alternative sources of financing. There are two types of ownership. There is legal ownership, and there is defacto ownership. Defacto ownership give the party with control all the benefits and none of the liabilities or responsibilities. This is a highly one-sided situation. Such a power imbalance is akin to slavery. This is clearly win-lose. The chances of this venture succeeding depend entirely on the benevolence of the party in the power position. It could go well, or not. In my experience, when there is such a large power imbalance, the outcome is rarely favorable. These arrangements survive for a very short period of time. Once the first point of stress hits, the partnership unravels very quickly.

Oops, I lost the company. It sounds crazy, and it is. However, it's surprisingly more common than you would think. I have witnessed two remarkably similar situations in less than two years. Incredibly smart people have made this simple mistake. I was evaluating another investment opportunity for a project in Louisiana. The company had signed a manufacturing agreement with a partner that gave the manufacturing partner an equity position. The manufacturer was going to fund the inventory of the product and act as the lender to fund the inventory. Here is the language from the operating agreement. The language in the body of the agreement was innocent enough. The land-mine was buried in the definitions section of the agreement.

"Controlling Vote of the Board of Managers" means the sole vote of the member of the Board of Managers elected by <Lender>until such time as all amounts due to <Lender> and/or any of its affiliates under the Joint Venture Agreement have been paid in full and thereafter, the vote of a Controlling Vote of the members of the Board of Managers.

With this definition, the lender had full control of the company, including the ability to issue more shares. There was no provision in the agreement to prevent dilution of share ownership. Therefore as soon as the company had even $1 of loan liability outstanding with the lender, the company had completely and irrevocably transferred control of the company to the lender. The worst part is the CEO of the company had no idea he given up control the company. When I read my interpretation of the language of the agreement to their senior management team, there was complete silence in the room. Silence was followed by denial. "That can't be! This lender is our friend. They're helping us out." Needless to say, we didn't invest in the venture. The project closed down as I had predicted because the company had lost control to the manufacturing partner.

Structure matters. It's the difference between success and failure.

Negotiating Win-Win

There are so many stakeholders involved in the success of a business venture. These include customers, employees, investors, partners. For the purpose of this discussion, we're going to confine the discussion to the dialog between the entrepreneur and the investors.

We'll assume that the operating budgets for the venture are agreed upon. The principles of the deal need to be spelled out on paper and agreed upon before you start drafting contracts.

I believe in win-win deals. I don't engage in win-lose deals, even if I'm on the winning side. They don't last the test of time. Eventually there will be a winner and a loser. Those deals always fail eventually. The best deals are the ones where everyone wins. In some cases, even with deals that started out structured as win-win, there can be failure situations where ultimately there is a winner and a loser. But we're not talking about that. If a business fails, then someone is going to get hurt. What I'm talking about is a structure where a successful business is forced prematurely into failure because of a win-lose structure.

Win-lose deals are based on scarcity mindset. The pie is only so large, so I'm going to get a larger slice of the pie at your expense. There is a very large percentage of the population who operate in this mindset. On the other hand, abundance mentality is more focused on making the pie bigger for everyone.

It starts with creating a term sheet for the venture. Let's look at an example.

Joe's Bakery

Let's imagine that you're starting a bakery. The investor is expected to fund the purchase of the equipment, facilities, and a few months of operating expense during which time the bakery builds its revenue base. In exchange, the investor is getting a 5% interest rate on their moneys as long as there is loan principal outstanding, and a 20% equity share of the business. The bakery is expected to be profitable by the end of six months. The owner of the bakery has delivered samples to a number of restaurants and grocery stores. The business plan calls for a business to business sales model, rather than the traditional business to consumer model. The business is expected to deliver a gross margin of 65%. That is to say, the direct variable cost of production represents 35% of the gross revenue. The remaining fixed costs are amortized over the volume of sales and should result in a net profit margin of 20% assuming the bakery meets its revenue targets. Under these conditions, the bakery should generate enough free cash flow to repay the investor in two years if 60% of the cash flow is allocated to repaying the investment. Once the loan is paid off, the preferred payment to the investor is terminated and the profits are shared according to share ownership.

Pro Forma Financial

Loan Principal	$750,000
Monthly Revenue	$260,417
Monthly Operating Expenses	$208,333
Monthly Interest Payable	$3,125
Monthly Profit	$52,083
Monthly Preferred Return to Lender	$31,250
Loan repayment (months)	24

The baker is happy. He's paying off the loan in exactly 24 months as agreed. The lender is happy. The business is generating a profit. Once the loan is repaid, the $52,083 in monthly profit is split according to ownership share. 80% goes to the owner for running the bakery each and every day. 20% or $10,416 every month goes to the funding partner and is mailbox money, residual income.

Here's what the financial project looks like when expressed in a term sheet.

TERM SHEET

Investment: $750,000

Interest rate: 5% annual.

Payment terms: Interest only paid monthly, principal

---

repaid through preferred return

Loan term: 2 years

Definition of Profit: Revenue minus Allowable Operating Expenses (defined), excluding any salary paid to business owner.

Preferred return: 60% of Profit

Conditions of default: Failure to pay interest when due, failure to repay loan in full within loan term.

Default Remedies: Shareholder pledges 50% of shares in the company in the event of default. Share certificates held in escrow.

Loan is immediately due on sale or change of control

There is a simple method for assessing whether a deal is win-win. I call this a sensitivity analysis. You start with a simple test case that is taken from the proposed pro-forma budget for the venture. The next step is to alter the financial projections **UP**and **DOWN** by an arbitrary 25%. By doing this you will be able to see the impact of the structure on the future outcome. This exercise can be extremely revealing. It can show you who the winners and losers are if the future unfolds differently from the initial plan. It's safe to say that the forecast will not be 100% accurate. It rarely is. We may not know how the future will deviate from the plan, only that it will. A good structure will accommodate the plan, an upside, and a downside.

In the case of 25% more revenue, life is good. The bakery generates nearly $75,000 per month in profit. The loan is repaid in 16.7 months. The baker is getting $29,948 per month in profit after paying back the preferred return to the loan principal.

25% More Revenue

Loan Principal	$750,000
Monthly Revenue	$325,520
Monthly Operating Expenses	$237,630
Monthly Interest Payable	$3,125
Monthly Profit	$74,870
Monthly Preferred Return to Lender	$44,922
Loan repayment (months)	16.7

Once the loan is repaid, the baker gets to keep 80% of the $74,870 in monthly profit, or $59,896. The investor is getting $14,974 each month. Again, everyone is happy.

Let's say that one of the restaurants backs out of the supply arrangement (a realistic scenario) and the revenue drops by 25%. The business is still profitable. Instead of generating $52,083 in profit each month, the bakery is generating $29,297 per month in profit. It's not as good as projected, but certainly not a disaster.

25% Less Revenue

Loan Principal	$750,000
Monthly Revenue	$195,312
Monthly Operating Expenses	$179,036
Monthly Interest Payable	$3,125
Monthly Profit	$29,297
Monthly Preferred Return to Lender	$17,578
Loan repayment (months)	42.7

Under this scenario, the loan would take 42.7 months to repay. The only problem is that the loan was negotiated with a 24 month term.

It is due and payable in full after 24 months. Every day after 24 months, the loan is in default. The terms of the agreement are such that 50% of the shares of the company are handed over to the lender in the event of default. The lender now owns 70% of the bakery, and the baker owns 30%. The lender is now going to make 70% of the $29,297 profit or $20,507 in profit share after the loan is repaid. The baker is working just as hard as before, and is making a meager $8,789 per month in profit.

Is this acceptable to all parties? Is it still win-win? Has it become win-lose?

It's not completely obvious. If I was the baker, I'd be unhappy under this scenario. Would the deal have been structured differently if the sensitivity analysis had been performed?

There could have been a loan renewal option added to the terms. If the bakery needed more than 24 months, then they could have paid a renewal fee on a percentage of the outstanding balance. The loan renewal could have been at a higher interest rate to compensate the lender for the longer loan term. It would have avoided the default scenario that would turn the venture into a win-lose situation. Needless to say, the baker would be much better off paying a few thousand dollars penalty to the lender, without losing control of the business. Anticipating these types of scenarios requires a little forethought.

Rights and Options – Two of the most powerful tools

I'm a huge fan of Rights and Options. In my view, these are some of the most powerful tools in deal structure and also the most under-utilized. The purpose of Rights and Options is to maintain control over a situation without necessarily having to spend any money. Let's look at a few cases of how these can be used to give an investor or a syndicator additional control.

RIGHTS

Let's say that I have set up a Limited Partnership. Limited Partners have a right to sell their shares and have someone else step into their shoes if they need to raise some cash in exchange for their interest in the partnership. If the other partners allow that to happen, they lose control over who the new partner may be. That new partner may not have the same values, or alignment of goals with the rest of the partners. This could become a source of conflict down the road. If, the Partnership Agreement gives a partner the right to sell, but also give the existing partners a RIGHT OF FIRST REFUSAL, then the seller still will get the same deal they had negotiated with the new buyer. But the existing partners would have the right to buy the shares under the same terms and maintain a greater element of control and ownership. The partners are not obligated to buy, but have the right. This is powerful.

Rights can be configured in a multitude of ways. The only limits are those of legality and the imagination.

OPTIONS

Even more powerful than Rights, Options can be used to maintain flexibility without spending a lot of cash. What is an option? It's simply an agreement that gives one party the choice. It's similar to a Right, and is often used when negotiating the purchase of an asset.

Example 1:

I could sign a three year commercial lease for an office, with an option to renew for another three years under the same terms. It's as if I have a six year COMMITMENT FROM the landlord, but I have only given a three year COMMITMENT TO the landlord. This creates an imbalance between the rights and responsibilities of the parties. It skews the flexibility in favor of the tenant. As a tenant, I can be secure in the knowledge that my office won't have to move for six years, but I could leave after three if I choose to.

Example 2:

Options can also be used to defer the cost of acquiring an asset. Let's imagine that I want to buy a parcel of land that's too large for me to develop all at once.

I may divide it in four and purchase only twenty-five percent of the land initially. I may then purchase a rolling option to buy the remaining land for the same price for, say, the next three years. If I purchase even one more parcel, we could agree that the three year expiration would reset to zero. Finally, if I don't purchase any land within the remaining three year timeframe, the option would expire.

Let's examine how this could benefit me financially.

- Land Purchase: $20,000,000
- Annual Property Taxes: $200,000
- Annual Interest charges on money borrowed: $1,000,000

In this scenario, the annual holding cost of the land is $1,200,000. In addition, as the owner, I'm carrying the full liability for the land even if I can't use it all at once.

- If I purchase the land in 25% increments with a rolling option,

  - Purchase of 1st 25% Parcel: $5,000,000
  - Annual Property Taxes: $50,000
  - Annual Interest Charges: $250,000
  - One Time Option Fee: $900,000

For the same $1,200,000 I can buy 25% of the land and maintain the option of buying the rest of the land for the next three years. But my carrying cost in the next two years is much lower and represents a saving of $900,000 per year for each of the next two years. During that time, the land owner can't sell the land to someone else, because I have the option, not them. If after the end of the three years, I decide that I don't want to buy the remaining land, I can simply walk away without being obligated to buy it. By having a rolling option, I can extend the purchase process up to twelve years by renewing the three year expiration date each time I purchase a parcel. Even though the price of $900,000 seems like a high price to pay for merely an option, the actual savings to the buyer can be substantial. It may also be a good deal for the seller. They know that they have a motivated buyer who has already invested $900,000 to tie up the property. The buyer won't walk away from that $900,000 investment lightly. Ultimately, the proceeds to the seller would be $21,900,000 and would be $900,000 higher than the original purchase price of $20,000,000. It seems like a win-win situation for both parties.

Successful Deal Structure is all about asking meaningful "What-if" questions. All projects start out with an expected outcome. If everything goes perfectly according to plan, then a simple negotiated deal makes perfect sense. However, the real world rarely gives us the expected outcome.

Ask numerous "What if" questions. What if:

- The project gets delayed?
- There are cost over-runs?
- The project is appraised for less than projected?
- A partner makes a financial error?

By engaging your team in critical scenario analysis like this, you will determine the best possible structure for your deal.

Final Thoughts

Raising capital is both an art and a science. The critical item is confidence. That confidence stems from the integration of the Five Principles discussed in this book. There must be a near-perfect fit between the goals of the entrepreneur and the goals of the investor. If that fit doesn't exist, it will be forced. Forced projects generally don't work.

But remember that you do have some flexibility to negotiate. The more investors you bring into a project, the less latitude you have to negotiate. Before you settle on a specific set of terms, solicit input from past investors, from your tax, legal and securities advisors, and other experienced entrepreneurs in your segment of the industry. This advice can save you lots of money, time, and heartache.

Don't feel compelled to do a deal, just because you're anxious to get a deal done. This often results in bad deals. Business is a long game. It's rarely won in a single project. The sustained compound effect of investment and return over a longer period is the ticket.

> *"We tend to over-estimate what we can do in a year, and tend to underestimate what we can accomplish in a decade."*
>
> Bill Gates

Appendix Recommended Readings

Klaff, Oren (January 2011). *Pitch Anything: An Innovative Method for Presenting, Persuading, and Sealing the Deal*, USA: Mcgraw-Hill.

Collins, Jim (October 2011). *Good to Great*, USA: Harper Business.

Covey, Stephen M. R (2006). *The SPEED of Trust: The One Thing that Changes Everything,* USA: Free Press.

Kawasaki, Guy (September 2004). *The Art of the Start*: *The Time-Tested, Battle-Hardened Guide for Anyone Starting Anything*, USA: Portfolio.

Weigel, Russell (January 2015). *Capital for Keeps: Limit Litigation Risk While Raising Capital*, New York, USA: Morgan James Publishing.

Fleishman, Joel Lawrence (January 2007). *The Foundation*, USA: Pubic Affairs.

ABOUT THE AUTHOR

Victor Menasce was born in Charlottetown, Prince Edward Island. He started his career in business at the age of 15, providing stage lighting and sound reinforcement for live theatre, and touring bands.

His family originated in New York City where his father was a dentist and his mother was a trail-blazing architect. She was the second woman in history to graduate in architecture from Cornell University and went on to build several landmark properties in Manhattan. It was here that Victor ignited his passion for building.

Victor graduated with a degree in electrical engineering. The early part of his career was spent designing microprocessor chips. He spent 25 years in the semiconductor and telecom industries and held senior roles in both private and public companies. During that time he was involved in teams that acquired several businesses. The skills needed to raise money were developed during those intense projects.

At age 45, he decided to take a career left turn and moved full-time into the world of real estate investment. Applying the universal principles of business, and experience amassed in over 15 different countries, Victor has been involved in nation-wide real estate projects.

Victor lives with his family in Ottawa, Canada.

You can reach Victor at:

victor@victorjm.com

Made in the USA
Columbia, SC
29 September 2020